A *Window* of *Grace*

Wesleyan Insights on Effective Prayer

Foreword By Donald E. Demaray

by Russell D. Jeffrey

A WINDOW OF GRACE
Russell D. Jeffrey

ISBN 0-89367-221-1

© 1997
Light and Life Communications
Indianapolis, IN 46253-5002
Printed in the U.S.A.

Dedicated to

Reverend Arthur H. Perry
"A Praying Saint"

Uncle Ralph;
You are an important part
of my life, even though our
paths don't cross to often.
Read this book with my
love & let God's love
flow through you.
I Love You
Sandra

Foreword

Pastor Rus Jeffrey hits the nail on the head when he quotes John Wesley as saying, "A Methodist is one who 'prays without ceasing.'" A Methodist's heart ever lifts "to God, at all times and in all places." And how does one get to that happy place of constant praying? Rus Jeffrey helps us get into the heart of John Wesley's discipline and style, his spirituality and his love for God. Entries from the journal of Methodism's founder, along with many prayers from his pen, help us catch the warmth and genius of Wesley on prayer.

For many years, Jeffrey has studied prayer with special attention to John Wesley. Now Jeffrey shares his findings in published form. The book will encourage Christians in earnest to get close to God. Some who pick up this volume have only skirted the edges of decision to know God intimately. Jeffrey's 60-day experiment will nudge readers to discover the riches of a spiritual life and the wealth that comes in the spirit of Wesley, who asked God to use him and all that he owned. Wesley surrendered himself totally to the Divine.

> "I do not belong to myself but to You. Claim me
> as Your right. Keep me as Your charge. Love me
> as Your child. Fight for me when I'm wounded.
> Revive me when I'm destroyed! Amen."

Donald E. Demaray
Professor — Asbury Theological Seminary
Autumn 1996

Introduction

One of the most often asked questions concerning prayer revolves around a concept probably evident since the beginning of time — How do I pray? After observing Jesus in prayer, the disciples approached Him saying, "Lord, teach us to pray." He, of course, did and gave them what's now known as the Lord's Prayer.

What is prayer? Simply stated, prayer is communication with a friend. What results from prayer? The opening of a window of grace. Through the avenue of prayer, one discovers not only answers, but also the wonderful grace God poured out onto His people. However, after saying this, we once again return to our original question — How do we pray?

The following pages aim at answering this question. Looking at prayer through the eyes of John Wesley we discover a very methodical system of approaching God in prayer. However, not only do we discover what one might call a Wesleyan approach to prayer, but we also find a biblically-based approach of opening this window of grace.

Through the use of a window motif we'll move through the process of establishing a life of prayer. Using Wesley as a starting point and mold, we'll move through various stages of life showing how the same method used by Wesley still holds true today. When looking at

John Wesley's first published prayers, one quickly discovers how relevant they were to the day in which he lived. This of course has not changed. Our prayers always revolve around the life we live.

The book itself is divided into two parts. Part one focuses on putting the frame and glass of the window in place. Part two challenges the reader to spend 60 days with Wesley. We can learn from his structure, then put it into practice in our lives today. The challenge? Spend 60 days following John Wesley's example, and then, once the form is firmly placed in your own prayer life, daily time with God will come more easily.

With a sense of joy I write these words of introduction. This prayer journey began at Asbury Theological Seminary while taking a class entitled *Wesleyan Spirituality* from Dr. Steve Harper. The outline started as a class paper. From there it kept growing as I spent more time looking at the pattern of prayer as outlined and lived by John Wesley. No magical formula will bring about a disciplined, firm and strong prayer life. However, I can tell you that the *window of grace*, known as prayer, has become more real to me as I have written these chapters.

May God bless you as you journey with Him and open His wonderful window of grace.

Rus D. Jeffrey
September 1996

Words of Thanks

First and foremost, I must thank and give all the praise and the glory to my Father in heaven. Without His help and guidance, none of this could have happened. He's taken ahold of my life, and I do humbly seek His will for my life with all my heart, soul, strength and mind. May this be a pleasing work unto Him.

Second, I need to say thanks to my wife, Sandra, and my three sons, Zack, Ryan and Benjamin. Boys, you watched Daddy spend many hours in his study, and I'm sure you wondered why at times. Now you know. Thanks for keeping the noise down to a dull roar — most of the time. Sandra, you probably wondered if I'd *ever* get this far! Here it is, sweetie! Now you don't have to worry about making late night coffee anymore.

Thanks to those who, through the months, read bits and pieces of chapters. I couldn't have done it without you. Your observations and input were greatly appreciated and put to good use in the many rewrites. I'd especially like to thank Lesley Peterson whose keen eye for grammar cleared up some mistakes before the manuscript finally made it to my editor.

Last but certainly not least, I must say thanks to editor Bob Haslam. What can I say, Bob? You've been patient, supportive, humorous and helpful all at the same time. I couldn't have done this without you or your weekly offerings of e-mail.

"A Window of Grace"

"Blown Away"

Lyrics by Laurie Leenhouts

Fresh breeze blow in
Through the windows of my heart.
Clear the webs
From the corners of my soul.
Replace the stale air
With a fragrance fresh and new;
Let the dust be blown away by You.

Blown away, blown away,
Let the dust be blown away.
Make my heart
A home that's fit for you.
Blown away, blown away,
By Your Spirit blown away,
Blown away,
By the presence of You.

A Window of Grace

Part One

A Time for Cleaning — The Importance of Prayer

"Love the Lord your God with all your heart and
with all your soul and with all your mind."
Matthew 22:37

A single light burns in an upper room at 5 a.m. From time to time a praying saint lightly hums a few bars of his favorite hymn, occasionally turning a page in a tattered and well-worn Bible. This preacher's day begins and ends right here, kneeling before God. The source of energy behind this remarkable servant of God is prayer. Driven by an unquenchable thirst for inward holiness, this evangelist pursues God the only way he knows how — on his knees. Without personal holiness, he believes, one cannot lead others in the noble pursuit of a holy life. The man in the upper room is John Wesley. Prayer for Wesley is not just an obligation. Prayer is a way of life.

Why is prayer so important? Are there not other ways for spiritual growth? The answer — yes and no. One may visit any Christian bookstore and discover literally hundreds of books about spiritual growth. However, if the avenue of prayer does not appear, one's spiritual journey becomes rough and results in little spiritual growth. Sometimes the path becomes so cluttered with *how tos*, that one actually loses sight of the real goal, a closer relationship with God.

Wesley discovered early in his journey, the most important book for spiritual growth is the Bible. Here, he found the glorious attributes of God, but his discoveries did not end there. Wesley also read the great prayers of people seeking God's heart. He noted the first cry: "At that time people began to invoke the name of the Lord" (Genesis 4:26, paraphrase). And he took notice of the final sigh: "The one who testifies to these things says; Surely I am coming soon. Amen. Come, Lord Jesus" (Revelation 22:20, paraphrase).

One finds many forms of prayer throughout the Bible. The Scriptures recount in great detail the spiritual journey of saints who lived long ago. As the story unfolds, we catch glimpses of the triumphs and struggles of early believers. Through one-to-one communication with God, these praying saints discovered God's will for their lives.

So where does this lead us? The ultimate answer lies in a life bathed in prayer. When looking at Christianity, one quickly realizes prayer must make up part of the spiritual journey. Christianity without prayer quickly becomes stagnant like pond water with no source of rejuvenation. Soon the pungent smell drives one away from God, instead of nearer.

John Wesley recognized this very important aspect of Christian life. In his book, *Devotional Life in the Wesleyan Tradition*, Steve Harper accurately describes Wesley as a "man of devotion."

When writing to an itinerant preacher concerning the importance of the devotional life, Wesley said: "O begin! Fix some part of every day for private exercises ... Whether you like it or not, read and pray daily. It is for your life; there is no other way: else you will be a trifler all your days."

A Source of Life

A source exists for everything. The glow of my computer screen finds its source of power in the socket found in the wall. The light guitar music filling my room begins from the spinning CD, which in turn sends music to the speakers. The well crafted music itself finds its source in the gifted Phil Keaggy.

As Christians we also seek a life source. C.S. Lewis believed that we catch a glimpse of our life source through nature. However, nature is only a symbol. Lewis encouraged us to pass beyond nature to the splendor which nature reflects. There, beyond nature, we discover God in all His glorious beauty.

However, like anything else, the source of life does not stand alone. Just as we depend on the source for life, the source depends on us for life. Harry Emerson Fosdick describes this unique relationship in *The Meaning of Prayer*.

"We ask the leaf, are you complete in yourself? The leaf answers, 'No, my life is in the branches.' We ask the branch, and the branch answers, 'No, my life is in the trunk.' We ask the trunk and the trunk answers, 'No, my life is in the root.' We ask the root, and it answers, 'No, my life is in the trunk and the branches, and the leaves. Keep the branches stripped of leaves and I shall die.'"

We find the source of life for Christianity in the heart of God. First Samuel gives an account of two anointed kings, Saul and David. However, there appears in this passage a major difference between these two people. At the anointing of Saul, God gave him a new heart. David, on the other hand, did not receive a new heart. When Samuel waited on God for direction in choosing a king he looked at the appearance of the man. God told Samuel He's not interested in what the king looks like; He's more concerned about the person's heart. When Samuel anointed David as king, he did not require a new heart because he already had a heart for God. Here we have a shepherd boy seeking the will of God in his life. David's heart provided the essential link between him and his Lord. His heart was already on fire for God.

In Wesley we also find a man seeking God with all his heart, soul and mind. Wesley knew the only hope for a corrupt heart was new birth. Once kindled, the fire stays aflame only when one remains in close contact with God. The avenue of prayer provides the path for this contact. Through prayer we discover the heart of God. Ultimately prayer provides the road leading to our source of life. Behind a heart on fire for God, we discover a heart nourished by prayer.

Through a Glass Darkly

When looking at the life of John Wesley, one quickly discovers a man spending hours in prayer. His daily journal entries record the spiritual journey of this prayer warrior. Wesley recorded, with the exactness of an Oxford professor, every facet of his daily life, devising his own shorthand. We find an example in his September 1733 journal. One entry simply says, "G. Tht 50." This particular morning Wesley spent time meditating on the words of Psalm 50.

Further investigation uncovers a series of *Ps* with various dashes above them. In his own subtle way Wesley recorded his perceived effectiveness during prayer. A straight line above a *P* indicated a standard time of prayer when nothing out of the ordinary occurred. A single line with a downward tail represented a time when Wesley felt his prayers did not break through. In actuality, he considered his prayers fallen down around him. Lastly, a straight line with an upward tail at the end of the dash indicated a time of extraordinary prayer. Here we catch a glimpse of joy as Wesley broke through to God in prayer.

Experiencing the presence of God, when one's prayers have truly taken wings and flown to His very heart, is a feeling hard to forget. But, prayer has its ups and downs. At times, praying comes easily and naturally; however, at other times prayer becomes difficult. Occasionally, one may see no use for prayer at all. Sometimes feelings of emptiness occur with a sense of praying in a vacuum where no sound seems to get out at all. Are these times when one should forget about prayer altogether? The answer, a resounding "No!" At times like these, when one feels abandoned by God, He may actually be nearer than you could ever imagine. Having a discipline of a daily devotional life in place before reaching this point helps a person in the area of persistence. Prayer through the hard times strengthens one's relationship with the Lord. When praying through the hard times, one actually discovers the hand of God reaching down from heaven and comforting hurts in a very special and powerful way.

Even the saints experience times of feeling distant from God. This should comfort anyone feeling like they're the first encountering distance. One night, while reading the journals of Francis Asbury, I came across a cry for a deeper walk with God. On October 11, 1774, Asbury wrote: "Last night my soul was greatly troubled for want of a closer walk with God. Lord, how long shall I mourn and pray, and not experience what my soul longeth for? And this day, my mind is nearly the same frame."

I found these words comforting, because at the time I, too, experienced dryness in my devotions. Reading the words of Francis Asbury helped me discover I am not alone in my struggles. Even great men like Francis Asbury struggled in prayer!

Even though there are times of dryness in prayer, there are other times when there's a sense one can reach out and actually touch the face of God. The key is not to give in and quit. Many times people stop praying altogether because they feel there's no use for prayer. Discipline and dialogue with God do not come overnight. Prayer is communication with God, and just like in any other relationship one must spend time building the relationship into a strong friendship. The benefits of such a relationship with God are treasures stored up in heaven. Such a relationship requires persistence.

Looking for God

Where does persistence in prayer lead? For John Wesley, the answer lies in one word — *holiness.* In his pursuit of holiness, Wesley's aim centered on the presence of God. His heart's desire was to think on God at all times. Wesley was so concerned with thinking on God at all times that one of his daily questions asked, "Did I think of God first and last?" Answering yes to such a question revolves around a life committed to prayer.

Wesley was not the first person to ponder the presence of God. Seventeenth-century monk Brother Lawrence discussed the idea of constantly seeking God in all we do at all hours of the day. In the book *The Practice of the Presence of God,* Brother Lawrence described his inner struggles. On some occasions he considered set devotional times as intrusions into his regular communication with God. He aimed for constant communication and constant devotion with his Lord. The basis for such a goal finds an anchor in a devotional life. William Law, one of John Wesley's spiritual mentors, commented on this saying, "Devotion signifies a life devoted to God."

For 60 years John Wesley sought God with all his heart, soul and mind. Prayer represents the avenue for this pursuit. Fueled by a desire for personal holiness, Wesley exhibited a passion for prayer. A desire sprang from his study of authors such as Thomas à Kempis, Henry Scougal and William Law. Under the influence of these great men of God, Wesley began his journey toward personal holiness, a road ultimately leading him to prayer. From a letter written in May

1765, we discover Wesley first read William Law's *Christian Perfection* and *Serious Call* in 1727. After reading these books, Wesley's resolution revolved around total devotion to God in body, soul and mind.

Devotion to God is grounded in a strong prayer life. Wesley recognized prayer as the lifeblood of Christianity. As a result, his entire life centered on prayer. He observed set devotional times every morning, afternoon and evening. Throughout the day, he prayed at least once every hour with what he called ejaculatory prayers. This does not mean he actually stopped everything for prayer. But he did make sure his mind centered on God and praised Him for whatever engaged him at that moment in time. John Wesley was so in tune with God that he could carry on a conversation with someone on the street and pray at the same time.

He once commented how prayer was more his business than anything else. In *The Character of a Methodist* Wesley described the effects of praying without ceasing. According to Wesley, lifting one's heart to God at all times and in all places constitutes true prayer. He viewed Methodists as people who think on God at all times. "Whether he lie down or rise up, God is in all his thoughts. He walks with God continually having the loving eye of his mind still fixed upon Him, and everywhere seeing Him that is invisible."

Conversation with a Friend

Bishop Jeremy Taylor served as another author influencing Wesley's spiritual journey. We find evidence of this in his sermon from Matthew 6:22-23. Wesley focused his hearers on the concept of a single eye for God. Quoting from Bishop Taylor's book *Rules of Holy Living and Dying*, Wesley said, "Simplicity and purity are the two wings that lift the soul up to heaven." Simplicity in intention and purity in affections. Without these two attributes, Wesley considered all endeavors after religion vain and ineffectual. The primary goal of the Christian is union with God. This is accomplished only through prayer. Total surrender requires living and loving God with all one's heart. What a blessing to know we can always be in the presence of God *even here on earth*!

Jesus illustrated simplicity of intention when He told His disciples they must be like children. A *childlike* faith does not mean a *childish* faith. My 4-year-old son depends on me for his needs. His childlike faith knows whatever he needs, I will provide. His childlike faith also knows when he falls down and hurts himself or is scared of the dark, he can come running to me and find protection in the arms of his father. His intentions are simple and basic. When he's scared or hurt, he comes with one idea in his mind, safety and comfort in my arms. This is the simplicity of intention Christians should exhibit when approaching God in prayer. When we are in need, or when we are hurting, God is always there. In Him we discover safety, love and warmth.

Affection sometimes considers what we *get* out of a relationship. This type of affection does not look for something in return. Just like the marriage covenant, purity of affection loves freely with no expectations. We don't pray in order to *get things*. We pray because the voice of God gently calls us to His side. When these two areas are in place, then and only then is our pursuit of holiness worthy. Of course, the only way to maintain simplicity of intention and purity of affection is through prayer.

In prayer, one discovers direct communication with God. Prayer opens the door for conversation with God through His Son Jesus. John Wesley recognized this and placed a strong emphasis on prayer in his personal life, as well as in the lives of the people with whom he ministered. Metaphorically speaking, Wesley said, "Prayer may be said to be the breath of our spiritual life. He that lives cannot possibly cease breathing." True prayer, says Wesley, is holy zeal coming from a calm, undisturbed soul, moved upon by the Spirit of God. This type of prayer moves mountains. This type of prayer changes not only the life of the person praying, but also touches the lives of many others ministered to by one who earnestly desires a deep and lasting relationship with God.

Traveling evangelist J. Edwin Orr tells a story of visiting Christ College, Oxford. With him was a young student named William Franklin Graham. They toured Christ College, pausing along the way to admire classrooms where many young scholars sat in the past. Imagine the sense of awe young Graham felt as they moved from room to room. The heritage and devotion permeating the air most surely filled them with reverence. After touring the classrooms, their interest turned to housing. In one set of rooms they found a desk and a single bed. Tucked off in a lone corner stood an altar rail.

Young Graham asked his mentor, "Whose place is this?"

The evangelist did not respond.

Graham asked again and again, "Whose room is this?"

Eventually the secret came out. The room they were standing in was where John Wesley lived as a student and professor. The young Graham was so moved by Wesley's room that he wanted to pray. Kneeling at the same altar rail where John Wesley knelt every day, Billy Graham prayed the now famous prayer, "Lord, do it again."

God moves mountains through the avenue of prayer. God brings revival in the life of His people through prayer. Prayer — communication with the Creator of life. Even though prayer is a natural act, this remains one of the hardest spiritual disciplines, because we live in a world where many distractions take our thoughts away from

God. However, this should not keep us from praying. Bill Hybel's book, *Too Busy Not to Pray*, addresses the fact that in today's fast-paced world, we must take time for prayer. An active prayer life is the key for spiritual growth. John Wesley knew this well. Many who went before him and have followed after him have discovered that the only way to follow Christ is to live a life grounded in prayer.

For Wesley, prayer presents a means of grace for the Christian. A means of grace represents a way in which one experiences the grace of God. As already mentioned, prayer provides the vital communication link between humankind and God the Father. In the high-tech world of today, many times people forget they can open this great window of grace and approach God in daily prayer. Are your windows in need of cleaning? This great window of grace is available for all Christians.

Some have allowed the windows to become clouded over with dirt, requiring attention. For others, the occasional smudge or streak has appeared. Whatever your case, I encourage you to take some time and begin cleaning off the window of grace known as prayer. Cleaning off the window marks the beginning of a great adventure and begins letting the Light of God shine through into one's life. Once this begins, a deeper relationship with the Lord can begin.

I invite you on a spiritual journey that will change your life.

CHAPTER TWO

Raising the Blinds —
A Lifetime of God's Calling

"Train a child in the way he should go,
and when he is old, he will not turn from it."
Proverbs 22:6

The Wesley Home

John Wesley was a man who possessed a passion for prayer. But where did this passion and life of discipline begin? Did it happen overnight? Some people point toward Wesley's childhood in the Epworth parsonage. Here a young Wesley observed daily the life of devotion modeled by his parents. Through the years, his love for God and the Bible grew stronger. A love that never left him.

In later years, Wesley remarked, "I am a man of one book and one book only." The book he referred to is the Bible. This love for Scriptures served as the guiding hand for all John Wesley believed, taught and preached. The significance of the Bible in the life of John Wesley comes as no surprise. His passion resulted from living in the Epworth parsonage where the Bible played a central role in every area of life. This was not a book shelved and dusted off once a week for Sunday services. The Bible was prominent in family prayers and in the private education of each Wesley child.

Susanna Wesley, sometimes referred to as the Mother of Methodism, lived a disciplined life of devotion before God. A discipline she in turn passed on to her children. As soon as the Wesley children could talk, Susanna taught them the Lord's Prayer, which they recited every morning and night. Soon they learned short prayers for their parents, and then later other forms of prayer helped. The devotional training did not end with prayers. Before long each Wesley child memorized scripture. All this took place before they could read.

Susanna Wesley also concentrated on the spiritual well-being of each child. In addition to six hours a week of formal education, Susanna set aside one hour a week for care of the soul. John's time came Thursday evenings. This left an indelible mark on young Wesley. In later years, when a fellow in Lincoln College, Oxford, John wrote his mother asking her to pray during the hour they had met on Thursday evenings. Here we detect the beginnings of a life dedicated to prayer. The roots of Wesley's time of prayer ran deep in his soul, prepared and nurtured by his mother.

The Annesley Home

Where did Susanna's zeal for the Word come from? No doubt the answer lies in her childhood. At the age of 13, Susanna already possessed a knowledge of some of the struggles within the church. This young preacher's daughter became interested in the ecclesiastical and doctrinal controversies of the day. She was the youngest of 25 children born to Nonconformist Dr. Samuel Annesley. Annesley, a Puritan minister who later was known as the St. Paul of the Nonconformist, enjoyed prominence as a preacher until the Restoration drove him away from his pulpit.

Reaching back to the life and childhood of Susanna, we recognize the burning heart for God aflame in her as well. She possessed the same zeal and love for a holy life she saw exhibited by her father. She in turn passed these Christlike characteristics on to her children, and John Wesley embodied all she taught and all she hoped for — children loving God with all their heart, soul and mind. In John Wesley we see the effects of multigenerational Christianity taking hold in the life of a child.

After leaving Epworth, John maintained close contact with his mother, corresponding many times through letters. In one letter Susanna revealed the secret of her deep spirituality which she in turn passed on to her son. Susanna wrote: "I will tell you what rule I observed, when I was young, and too addicted to childish diversions — never spend more time in any matter of mere recreation in one day than I spent in private religious duties."

How much time do we waste today in *mere recreation?* A startling thought, and no doubt a large number of hours if one stops and ponders this question for long.

Time Usage

Wesley spoke a great deal concerning idle time. He considered idle time a sin. If one sits idle, he or she should think of God at the same time. In our fast-paced world today this is a difficult concept. We live in a world of instants. There's instant coffee, instant cereal and instant news capturing headlines of the day. There's even instant recreation! People power walk and power jog. Some even refer to power naps! If you ask someone to slow down and smell the roses, you're considered a lunatic in some places.

In this world of instants, there's even instant religion. Preachers talk of presenting a 10-minute gospel. The attention span of the normal person sitting in a pew on any given Sunday is now clocked around 15 minutes. People remember sermons only if the preacher entertains and hits the high points, finishing before the pot roast burns at home. God forbid if the sermon goes over by five minutes, because watch alarms begin ringing all over the room, and people start pointing at the time.

While looking through the shelves of a bookstore one day I discovered a book entitled *The 60 Second Devotion*. My heart broke with the realization that God is being strategically regulated out of the lives of many Christians. In a world of instants, God is pre-empted by the latest hit TV show. God is now no more than a 60 second commercial, and in some people's eyes, this is nothing more than an occasion for a trip to the refrigerator.

So, where does John Wesley fit in today? In Wesley we observe the struggle of maintaining a balanced devotional life with all the other cares of the world. I realize we cannot go back to the 18th century, and I'm not proposing this as a solution. But I refuse to believe we should regulate God to nothing more than a 60 second commercial break.

I remember a small charm my mother had on her dresser when I was a child. It always fascinated me, and I loved reading the words over and over again.

God gave us six days of the week to do whatever we please. The least we can do is give Him one hour on the seventh day.

As a young child, I thought these words carried great wisdom. I tried living them out as well. Every Sunday my mother would rise early and get the family up and dressed in our Sunday best. From time to time my brothers and I would complain saying we didn't want to go. But come Monday morning my mind would wander to the words of the charm, and I'd feel like I'd just cheated God out of His hour.

I look back on those days and ponder the wisdom of the now misplaced charm. My parents have moved from my childhood house and now live in an apartment. Going home just doesn't quite seem the same. Home is the place in which I grew up. Home is where I first learned about giving time to God. Here the seeds were planted for a life of devotion. I often wonder where the charm is — all I have now is the memory of a somewhat tarnished piece of metal with wise words engraved on it, words I often heard my mother tell me. Words that still ring with a certain sense of truth.

Yes, God did graciously give us the days of the week. However, I've also come to realize I need to give Him much more than just one hour of my life per week.

Fond Memories

I'm sure John Wesley's mind often traveled back to the days in the Epworth parsonage. His mind also traveled to the wise words of his mother. Devotion to God is the most important aspect of anyone's life. The key for Christian growth is prayer. This was a lesson John Wesley learned well. His aim was the pursuit of holiness.

God calls us to be a holy people. Wesley took this call seriously and devoted his entire life to searching for a deeper relationship with God. John Wesley has left us a pattern. His is not the only pattern to God, but I believe it is a very useful one. This pattern is useful because it always points up toward God. The source of life is found in the heart of God.

No one ever said a life of devotion is an easy one. A disciplined prayer life does not come easily. Even Jesus' disciples struggled in this area. Matthew tells of the disciples' falling asleep during the last hours of Christ's life. Jesus asked, "Could you men not keep watch with me for one hour? ... The spirit is willing, but the body is weak" (Matthew 26:40-41). During His final hours, the disciples were overcome with sleep and could not stay awake and pray.

Prayer is one of the most natural acts a human can perform. God the Father gently calls us to His side daily. Imagine the days in the Garden when God walked in the cool of the day and called Adam and Eve to His side (Genesis 3:8). Not only do we yearn for communication with God, but God Himself desires this for us. He calls us and wants to speak with us.

However, there was that fateful day in the Garden when Adam and Eve hid from God (Genesis 3:9). But, even though sin entered humanity, communication with the Father remains a natural act. As a matter of fact, since the beginning of time, when Adam and Eve were banished from the Garden, God has been calling His people back to His side.

I remember a time not too long ago when prayer was somewhat difficult for me. Finding myself in the midst of what seemed like many hopeless situations, I wondered if my prayers were actually getting through to God in the morning. One day while sitting at my desk, I looked up at the closed curtains and drawn blinds on my window. Thinking out loud I said, "God, that's kind of how I feel right now. I feel like I'm praying and looking for direction, but my prayers aren't getting through because You have the curtains and blinds closed." With the words still hanging in the air, I reached up, took hold of the pull strings, opening the curtains and blinds, allowing the morning sunlight to fill the room. "There," I thought to myself, "let's try this again, God."

How has God been calling you? All of us can look into the past and discover the hand of God on our lives in one form or another. He's been gently calling each one to His side so all humankind may experience the fullness of life. God speaks to us, and we speak to Him through prayer. Let's raise the blinds of our lives, and discover

God's hand at work. Once the blinds have been raised, we're ready for a deeper walk with Him.

Framing the
Glass — Written Prayers

"This, then, is how you should pray:
'Our Father in heaven, hallowed be your name, your
kingdom come, your will be done on earth as it is in
heaven. Give us today our daily bread. Forgive us our
debts, as we also have forgiven our debtors. And lead us
not into temptation, but deliver us from the evil one.'"
Matthew 6:9-13

Which has more power? A prayer prayed in
silence and awe of Whom we're standing
before or a prayer spoken loudly using all
kinds of $25 theological words? Both are effective. However, most
people pray timidly as opposed to loudly.

One complaint early Methodists held against Anglicans revolved around the issue of forms of prayers. Great concern arose over
the matter of written prayers versus free flowing prayers from a person's
heart.

One story tells of a meeting between a Methodist preacher
and an Anglican priest on the streets of London in which the Methodist gentleman decided he would set the Anglican straight concerning
their cold and boring prayers. Pulling him to one side this well meaning preacher commented, "The problem with you Anglicans is you
don't really know how to pray. All you do is look at written prayers."

The Anglican priest calmly replied, "That's where you're

mistaken my good friend. It is true, our prayers are in written form. However, when we read these prayers, we actually *pray* them from the heart."

One of the most often asked questions concerning prayer centers on: "What are the right words?" Others ask: "Why would God in heaven want to talk to me? If He already knows what's going on, who am I to do anything?" If you struggle in prayer, have no fear. Most people do struggle when attempting to find the right words. Some feel embarrassed about asking that question. However, I'd like to point out that whoever asks ends up in good company, because almost 2,000 years ago the disciples asked the very same question by saying, "Lord, teach us to pray."

Popular Misconceptions

Through the years we've been silently trained by others around us concerning the language of prayer. Of course, through the centuries various thoughts of just *who* should pray have arisen as well. What's interesting is how misconceptions sometimes turn into popular truths.

Many times when a pastor asks a layperson to pray, the response can be somewhat shocking. With great sincerity, the person replies saying, "No, that's your job." Of course, the idea that prayer is for special people erodes the motive for prayer. There are still others who pray for the little things in life, but when the going gets tough, the pastor becomes the designated "pray-er." Others become embarrassed praying in public. What happens if I lose my train of thought or say the wrong thing, are common concerns.

What do these stories tell us? They reveal the tendency in people to paint a picture of prayer as an exercise for those who are especially spiritual or those who are professionally trained. However, when looking at the Lord's Prayer, we discover a different picture. The prayer given by Jesus was in direct response to the request, "Lord, teach us to pray."

Just who were the *us?* They were the disciples, none of whom were professionally trained. Instead they were fishermen, tax collectors and political revolutionaries. They were the women who followed Jesus and the common people who gladly heard the good news of the kingdom of God. The ones who asked Jesus the simple question of how to pray were plain, ordinary, everyday people seeking a deeper communication level with the Father in heaven. They were the kind of people you and I are today.

If only special people could pray, Jesus never would have taught the Lord's Prayer. Instead, when answering the question He would have said, "Don't worry about prayer. Just tell me what you want, and I'll pray for you." After all, Jesus is the Son of God, and surely if anyone can get through to God, He can.

The Lord's Prayer

What do we discover by looking closer at the Lord's Prayer? On the surface, one quickly notices how Jesus illustrated that prayer is for everyone, with no hierarchy. In Matthew He responded by saying, "This is how you should pray ..." (Matthew 6:9). In the Luke passage Jesus simply says, "When you pray say ..." (Luke 11:2). Prayer is for everyone. As we approach the throne of grace with prayers on our hearts and lips, there is no distinction between first class and second class. This great window of grace remains open for all who call His name.

Outside of "Now I lay me down to sleep ...," the Lord's

Prayer probably represents one of the first prayers children learn. Of course, as always happens, sometimes children miss out on the language and simply insert what they think they hear. While saying her bedtime prayers with her mother one night, a little girl said, "Dear Harold, please bless Mother and Daddy and all my friends, amen."

"Wait a minute," interrupted her mother, "who's Harold?"

"That's God's name," replied the little girl.

"Now who told you that was God's name?" asked the mother.

"I learned it in Sunday school, Mommy," came the excited reply. "It's how the Lord's Prayer starts. 'Our Father, who art in heaven, Harold be thy name.'"

Some people ask why we should even bother with the Lord's Prayer. After all, so the argument goes, the Lord's Prayer has lost all meaning through the years. How can a prayer taught by Jesus some 2,000 years ago hold relevancy for us today? I must admit, in some instances this is true. I've attended services where people have prayed the Lord's Prayer with about as much energy and meaning as a person who's just received anesthetic for a major surgical operation!

A professor once compared the sliding from one extreme to another with that of a ship rocking back and forth at sea. If everyone on the ship gathers on the same side, the ship begins tipping in that direction. Reacting to the sensation of capsizing the ship, everyone quickly runs to the opposite side of the ship. This of course results in the same sensation of falling overboard; however, this time it's in the opposite direction. Amazingly enough, very few people stop at the center of the ship where a proper balance is discovered.

Now let's apply this same illustration to our discussion of the Lord's Prayer. We find our balance in the very words of Jesus in the Gospels. Here we discover our starting and ending point. Through the years, however, one of two things happens. Either the Lord's Prayer takes on the cardboard feeling of flat meaningless words repeated strictly from memory with no consideration of meaning at all, or the Lord's Prayer becomes forgotten altogether.

I must admit at times I've fallen into the latter category. I'll never forget the day this realization really hit home. While sitting in a restaurant one morning for breakfast, a group of people who'd just started attending the church I pastored asked the simple question, "Why don't you say the Lord's Prayer during your services?"

The restaurant owner looked over her coffee pot somewhat astonished exclaiming, "What! You mean *you* don't say the Lord's Prayer?!"

Caught a little off guard, I didn't know how to respond. Quickly running through all the excuses I'd learned in "Scape-Goating 101" at seminary, I responded, "Well, to put it plain and simple — I just forget most of the time."

You could have heard a pin drop in the room that day. After all, here was a preacher saying he just forgets to say the Lord's Prayer! I don't forget the words, but I just simply forget to pray it. I'm not sure why this happens, but it does. One reason could revolve around the fact that when I was a child, we always said it at church. Through the years the prayer turned into nothing more than a simple collection of words.

Life to Written Words

Bring life to the written word. In radio it's known as theater of the mind. Capturing one's imagination, bringing life to what may originally seem hard and stiff. How does one bring life to a prayer spoken almost 2,000 years ago? At some point the prayer must become relevant for the person praying. The entire Lord's Prayer must be something flowing out of a truly committed heart.

We cannot pray "our" if we're living only for ourselves.

We cannot pray "Father" if we do not try each day to act like a child of God.

We cannot pray "who art in heaven" if we're more concerned with the earthly realm of life as opposed to treasures in heaven.

We cannot pray "hallowed be Thy name" if we're not seeking His face each day truly striving after holiness.

We cannot pray "Thy kingdom come" if we're not doing all that's within our power to bring that glorious day one step closer.

We cannot pray "Thy will be done" if we are disobedient and ignore His Word.

We cannot pray "in earth as it is in heaven" if we're not serving Him here and now in the present.

We cannot pray "give us this day our daily bread" if we're living dishonest lives or seeking fulfillment with a backup plan always in place.

We cannot pray "forgive us our debts" if we harbor a grudge against anyone.

We cannot pray "lead us not into temptation" if we're deliberately placing ourselves in its path.

We cannot pray "deliver us from evil" if we're not putting on the whole armor of God.

We cannot pray "Thine is the kingdom" if we are not giving the King the loyalty due Him from faithful servants.

We cannot attribute to Him "the power" if we're living in fear of what others may do to us.

We cannot attribute to Him "the glory" if we're seeking honor only for ourselves.

Lastly, we cannot pray "forever" if the horizon of our lives is bound completely by earthly time concepts.

Bringing new life to written words is not always an easy task. As a matter of fact, a major stumbling block for many beginning in prayer revolves around the whole area of finding the right words. Many believe it's a magical formula. Others believe you must always pray written prayers. Still others believe God is only present when a person prays totally from the heart with no regard to written prayers at all. Finding the right words for prayer does not present a new problem. The language of prayer has been a problem since the beginning of time.

Searching for Reality in Prayer

John Wesley struggled with the same question of how to pray. Caught in the midst of a system using the *Book of Common Prayer*, Wesley sought a balance between the written form and a heart after God. How could one simply read written prayers, while at the same time maintaining a heart seeking after God? How could one simply seek God through prayer, if in turn there was no pattern to the prayer? Here lies the struggle of bringing reality to one's prayer life.

Just how important was this issue for John Wesley? Important enough that his first publication, written at the age of 30, was a book entitled *A Collection of Forms of Prayer*. For many years this important work of Wesley's has been either overlooked or totally forgotten. These prayers, first compiled in 1733, and revised nine times after that up until the year 1755, reflect Wesley's devotional life and method of personal prayer.

Recognizing the struggle for reality in one's prayer life, he first prepared his book of prayers for use by his University group at Oxford. From these prayers of 1733, one quickly learns of the needs, aspirations and spiritual quality of those first using them. Wesley comments in his *Journal* from that year, "I printed, the first time I ventured to print anything, for the use of my pupils, *A Collection of Forms of Prayer*. In this I spoke explicitly of giving the whole heart and the whole life to God."

The first aspect of Wesley's Holy Club that impressed the critics was the disciplined habits of the group itself. The members of this group spent regular time in prayer. John Wesley himself devoted from five to six every morning and evening for the specific purpose of prayer. The Oxford Methodists were characterized by their disciplined life of reading the Scriptures, attending worship service, receiving communion, and regular, daily times of prayer. All of this was done for the specific reason of seeking God with their whole life.

When people wonder how and why the Methodist revival began, we can look at the disciplined prayer and devotional life of the founder, John Wesley. Behind the organization was a system of devotional faith. This devotional faith formed the basis, structure and foundation of lives firmly built on the solid foundation of Jesus Christ. As we finish framing the glass for a life of prayer, it seems only fitting that we conclude this chapter with the preface of John Wesley's first published work, *A Collection of Forms of Prayer*.

The Preface to Wesley's First Collection of Prayers

"The intention of the collector of these prayers was, first, to have forms of prayer for every day in the week, each of which contained something of deprecation, petition, thanksgiving and intercession. Secondly, to have such forms for those days which the Christian church has ever judged peculiarly proper for religious rejoicing, as contained little of deprecation, but were explicit and large in acts of love and thanksgiving. Thirdly, to have such for those days, which from the age of the Apostles have been set apart for religious mourning, as contained little of thanksgiving, but were full and express in acts of contrition and humiliation. Fourthly, to have intercessions every day, for all those whom our own church directs us to remember in our prayers. And fifthly, to comprise in the course of petitions for the week, the whole scheme of our Christian duty.

"Whoever follows the direction of our excellent church in the interpretation of the Holy Scriptures, by keeping close to that sense of them which the Catholic Fathers and ancient Bishops have delivered to succeeding generations will easily see that the whole system of Christian duty is reducible to these five heads.

"First, the renouncing ourselves: 'If any man will come after me, let him renounce himself and follow me.' This implies, first, a thorough conviction that we are not our own; that we are not the proprietors of ourselves, or any thing we enjoy; that we have no right to dispose of our goods, bodies, souls, or any of the actions or passions of them. Secondly, a solemn resolution to act suitably to this conviction; not to live to ourselves, not to pursue our own desires, not to please ourselves, nor to suffer our own will to be any principle of action to us.

"Such a renunciation of ourselves naturally leads to the devoting of ourselves to God. As this implies, first, a thorough conviction, that we are God's, that He is the proprietor of all we are, and all we have. And that not only by right of creation, but of purchase. For He died for all. And therefore died for all, that they which live, should not henceforth live unto themselves, but unto Him that died for them. Secondly, a solemn resolution to act suitably to this conviction. To live unto God, to render unto God the things which are God's, even all we are, and all we have, to glorify Him in our bodies, and in our spirits, with all the powers, and all the strength of each, and to make His will our sole principle of action.

"Thirdly, self denial is the immediate consequence of this. For whosoever has determined, to live no longer to the desires of men, but to the will of God, will soon find that he cannot be true to his purpose, without denying himself, and taking up his Cross daily. He will daily feel some desire which this one principle of action, the will of God, does not require him to indulge. In this therefore he must either deny himself, or so far deny the faith. He will daily meet with some means of drawing nearer to God, which are unpleasing to flesh and blood. In this therefore he must either take up his Cross, or so far renounce his Master.

"Fourthly, by a constant exercise of self-denial, the true follower of Christ continually advances in mortification. He is more and more dead to the world, and the things of the world, until at length he can say, with that perfect disciple of his Lord, I desire nothing but God, or with St. Paul, I am crucified unto the world, I am dead with Christ, I live not, but Christ lives in me.

"Fifthly, Christ lives in me. This is the fulfilling of the law, the last stage of Christian holiness. This makes the man of God perfect, he that being dead to the world is alive to God, the desire of whose soul is unto his name, who has given him his whole heart, who delights in Him and in nothing else but what tends to Him. Who for his sake burns with love to all Mankind, who neither thinks, speaks, nor acts, but to fulfill his will, is on the last round of the ladder to heaven, grace has had its full work upon his soul. The next step he takes is into glory.

"May the God of glory give unto us who have not already attained this, neither are already perfect, to do this one thing, forgetting those things which are before, to press toward the mark for the prize of our high calling in Christ Jesus.

"May He so enlighten our eyes, that we may reckon all things but loss, for the excellency of the knowledge of Christ Jesus our Lord, and so establish our hearts that we may rejoice to suffer the loss of all things, and count them but dung, that we may win Christ."

John Wesley — 1733

Additional Opening to Third Edition Preface

"The following Collection of Prayers, is designed only for those who, by the mercy of God, have, first leisure and resolution to set apart at least half an hour twice a day, for their private addresses to Him, and secondly, a sincere reverence for, if not some acquaintance with, the ancient Christian church. He who has not the former qualifications, will take offense at the length. He who has not the latter, at the matter of them."

John Wesley — 1738

Stained Glass — A Pattern for Devotion

"Be perfect, therefore, as your
heavenly Father is perfect."
Matthew 5:48

We have a stained glass name sign hanging in our front window. It's made of different shades of blues, and when the sun shines through, scattered colors run around the carpet. One day my sister-in-law looked at the sign and commented, "What a nice sign. What does it say?"

Not missing a beat I quickly replied, "Smith."

"Oh, that's nice," she said quietly.

We carried on throughout the day with family activities and later in the evening walked out to the car for our goodbyes. Looking up at the window my sister-in-law discovered what the sign really said.

"That doesn't say Smith, it says Jeffrey!"

Imagine that, I thought to myself, a name sign with *our* name on it.

Stained glass has always fascinated me. I've never tried my hand at it. But, I've seen a few people work at it — the careful knife cuts, grinding, sanding and soldering, and in some cases, even antiquing the piece. Stained glass can be as easy as piecing together four or five pieces for a lamp shade. Or as complicated as piecing together a name sign like Jeffrey. For every bend of a letter, there must be a corresponding break. This of course means that for every corresponding break, there is another break or two in the backdrop.

To give you an example, the name Jeffrey contains 26 breaks alone. This does not include breaks in the backdrop. The man who made our sign calculated it would take some 80 to 90 pieces to make it! As a result, he did something just a little different. Instead of making our name part of the backdrop, he first cut out the 26 pieces for our name. Then he designed a single piece for the backdrop in the shape of a scroll. With the one piece backdrop, he carefully attached the name pieces to the sign. It looks great, and unless you get right up on top of the sign, you can't tell the backdrop is only one piece.

When we picked up the completed sign, the gentleman who made it warned us he didn't know how long the name would stay attached. After all, even though it looks like a great stained glass name sign, it's really an imitation where some short cuts were taken. The name pattern hasn't actually become part of the entire work. In other words, all the pieces have not become one.

The Importance of Pattern

Step number one in the project of making a stained glass work is the pattern. The artist first sketches the pattern on paper, then lays a piece of glass over the pattern so it can be cut into the proper shape. A pattern for prayer can be described in the same fashion.

The imagery of stained glass gives us a pattern for devotion. Of course, many questions arise at this point. Just how does one put the pattern into place? Does this mean simply reading a set of prayers over and over again with no connection to the life we're living? With what written prayers do we begin? Why do we need a pattern at all? These are good questions, and I'm sure there are many more. But I want to focus on the last question — Why do we need a pattern at all?

Before arriving where we want to end up, it's important to know the directions. Bouncing aimlessly around only results in confusion and a sense of hopelessness. We must first ask — Where are we heading? If we're heading for a deeper relationship with God, this means our stained glass pattern must include a life of prayer. Prayer is the language one uses when communicating with God.

Do we merely lay prayers on top of our lives in the hope we will somehow communicate with the Lord by using another person's prayers? Not exactly. Simply reciting the prayers of others is like the shape of our name sign. On the surface it appears as though everything is intact. However, a closer look reveals the prayers are merely attached to the surface. They haven't taken root in the life of the person who is praying.

When seeking God, pattern is important, because this helps one focus. However, finding a pattern that fits well with an individual can be a challenge. So, how do we discover the best fit? We do so by looking at existing patterns and then making them our own. Many people recognized the Wesley brothers and the Holy Club as a group of people seeking God's heart and will for their lives through a disciplined life of prayer. As a result they were given the name *Methodists*. Of course the nickname *Methodist* was not an endearing one when first used as a description for this group.

The Holy Club or Oxford Club found themselves given this name by people making fun of them. The name Methodist was no doubt thrown at them as they walked down the hall. "There go those *Methodists* again. Who do they think they are anyway?" But, they could become so methodical in their approach to God that they might miss Him as a result of the very method they use.

Righteous Over Much

Missing God through the method used? Is this possible? Should this be a concern? John Wesley found himself asking the same questions. One of my favorite Wesley letters is not one in which he proclaimed some deeply profound spiritual truth. Nor is it one in which he reported the conversion of hundreds of new believers after a time of preaching. No, my favorite letter is one addressed to his mother in which he wonders if he's worrying much over little. I often think to myself "Yes, Mr. Wesley, you were a perfectionist." But what led him to this concern?

To his mother Wesley wrote, "When we were with him, (Mr. Kirkham), we touched two or three times upon a nice subject, but did not come to any full conclusion. The point debated was, What is the meaning of being *righteous over much,* or by the more common phrase of being *too strict in religion?* and what danger there was of any of us falling into that extreme?

"All the ways of being too righteous or too strict which we could think of, were these: Either the carrying some one particular virtue to so great a height, as to make it clash with some others; or, the laying too much stress on the instituted means of grace, to the neglect of the weightier matters of the law; or, the multiplying prudential means upon ourselves so far, and binding ourselves to the observance of them so strictly, as to obstruct the end we aimed at by them, either by hindering our advance in heavenly affections in general, or by retarding our progress in some particular virtue. Our opponents seemed to think my brother and I [were] in some danger of being too strict in this last sense; of laying burdens on ourselves too heavy to be borne, and, consequently, too heavy to be of any use to us.

"It is easy to observe, that almost every one thinks that rule totally needless which he does not need himself; and as to the Christian spirit itself, almost every one calls that degree of it which he does not himself aim at, enthusiasm. If therefore we plead for either, (not as if we thought the former absolutely needful, neither as if we had attained the latter,) it is no great wonder that they who are not for us in practice should be against us. If you, who are a less prejudiced judge, have perceived us faulty in this matter, too superstitious or enthusiastic, or whatever it is to be called; we earnestly desire to be speedily informed of our error, that we may no longer spend our strength on that which profiteth not. Or whatever there may be on the other hand, in which you have observed us to be too remiss, that likewise we desire to know as soon as possible. This is a subject which we would understand with as much accuracy as possible; it being hard to say which is of the worse consequence, — the being too strict, the really carrying things too far, the wearying ourselves and spending our strength in burdens that are unnecessary, — or the being frightened by those terrible words, from what, if not directly necessary, would at least be useful."

John Wesley — June 11, 1731

Wesley recognized the path to Christian perfection, not absolute perfection, was one involving a life of prayer. He knew this also included a methodical and disciplined approach to one's personal relationship with God. At the same time, however, he also recognized the pitfalls of becoming *righteous over much* or *too strict in religion*. Of course that is exactly the concern he's expressing to his mother in his letter of 1731. In their disciplined and methodical life, John and his brother Charles were aiming at a right relationship with God. However, some were saying the way in which they conducted themselves in the discipline of aiming at that relationship was actually taking them further away from God.

As a result of the conversation with Mr. Kirkham, Wesley approached his mother for advice concerning the method in which they were pursuing God. From the letter, we get the strong sense that the last thing Wesley wanted to be accused of was being too strict and missing the goal of God. We "plead," wrote Wesley, for your direction on this concern. If the practice is against us, let us know. We do not know how Susanna Wesley responded, but if she did, she must have responded in a positive manner because the method of the Methodists continued.

Spiritual Gift or Discipline

I once heard a story of a young mother who tried in vain to get her son to eat his dinner. After repeatedly refusing to eat what she'd prepared, the mother finally asked her son what he would like to eat. Trying to be as difficult as he could, the boy finally replied, "I want a worm to eat!"

The mother had recently been reading some psychology books and just finished a chapter explaining how children should be given exactly what they ask for. So looking at her husband, she asked him to go to the garden and find a worm. The father did so, but the son was still dissatisfied. He complained that he wanted the worm cooked. His mother promptly tossed the worm into a boiling pot of water and cooked it. After the worm was cooked she set it on the table in front of the young boy. However, once again it was the same old story of refusal.

"Now what?" asked the mother.

The boy said he wanted his father to eat half of the worm first. Still believing in the idea that the child should have his way, the father reluctantly ate half the worm. No sooner had this been done when the boy let out a tremendous scream of dissatisfaction.

"Daddy ate the half I wanted!!"

Have you ever noticed how sometimes even when we get our way, we still find excuses for not doing what we should? Prayer is the only way of communicating with God. However, the sad realization is, prayer has become a forgotten discipline. As long as there are people in need of God, prayer will always be evident, but one of two things happens. Either prayer becomes an afterthought and is done only when the going gets tough, or prayer happens so quickly that one's mind doesn't slow down before it gets cranked up again for the next task of the day. We must not only find time to pray, but we must also make the time and then stick to it.

I've often used the analogy of a car when describing the importance of a disciplined prayer life. Let's say you need milk from the store. You pull on your shoes, head out the door, jump in the car and let it coast down onto the road. You then drive to the store, and once you're there, you finally decide to turn the key in the ignition so the car will start.

Is this what you do? Of course not. Once you're in the car the first thing you do before putting the car in gear is turn the key in the ignition so it will start. In order for the car to move down the road, it needs the power from the engine. The engine is powered up only after the key is turned in the ignition. I'm afraid there are many people walking around every day in coast mode because they haven't tapped into the power of God through morning prayer.

One day after using this illustration, someone described a pastor with the gift of evangelism. They said how he had an extroverted personality, was very outgoing and very personable. He constantly got on other pastors' cases for not doing more evangelism. He thought something coming so easy to him should also come easy for everyone else. On the other hand, this same gentleman struggled with devotions and prayer. This discussion, of course, led up to a reason for *not* praying on a regular basis. After all, maybe a person just isn't gifted in the area of prayer.

On the surface this sounds reasonable, but it's kind of like having the father eat the wrong half of the worm. One should never expect others to be strong in the same spiritual gifts he possesses. Not everyone has the gift of evangelism. Prayer, however, does not fall under this category. A person with the spiritual gift of evangelism, or any other spiritual gift, should not browbeat others into his mold. Prayer is not a spiritual gift given to some and not to others. Quiet time with the Lord on a daily basis is a requirement for spiritual growth, not an option. If a person is not healthy in this area of life, he will not be healthy in other areas, which may even fall under the category of spiritual gifts. In a regular and disciplined quiet time with the Lord we discover more and more about Jesus and His meekness. As a result, we in turn give up more and more of our own selves.

The monastic tradition provides another methodical approach to a life seeking the heart of God. Trappist Monk Thomas Merton explains how we seek after what we do not know, and we actually seek after it in ways we do not know. As soon as we think we've found it, we've stopped thinking about what God wants for us, and we've started thinking about what we want Him to look like. We must always be dying to self, and the only way we can do this is by spending time with Him.

We must remember, of course, that we're all different. It's true, some people are not morning people. Of course, those same people who aren't morning people probably stay up rather late at night. The first question one should ask is, *What's keeping me from quiet time with the Lord?* Once this question is answered, the discipline can begin.

The bottom line is we live in a world where many people skirt around the issues. The Oxford boys were called the Holy Club and Methodists for a reason. They methodically planned out how they could pursue a life of holiness. The method they chose was a life of disciplined actions all seeking God. Through the years, Wesley has been misread at times as being nothing more than a legalist ogre. Such statements overlook letters like the one he wrote to his mother voicing his concern about possibly being righteous over much. If John Wesley were only concerned with the form and discipline, he would not have written his mother expressing worry about possibly missing the mark of Christ as a result of too much method.

The truth of the matter is that God wants us to come to Him daily bringing our offerings and sacrifices to Him. We do so through the avenue of prayer. Quiet time with God is a discipline, a discipline that must be made, and a discipline that is, even at different times in life, harder or easier for some. Sometimes when people recognize *why* they struggle, then the solution, or discipline, comes easier to follow through.

In 1959 Catherine Marshall found herself newly remarried and trying to raise three stepchildren. With much to pray about, she and her husband Len LeSourd could not find time to pray. Finding themselves at the end of their rope and recognizing the need for a disciplined prayer life, they began the coffee pot experiment. An automatically timed percolator coffee pot aromatically woke them up every morning at 6. Feeling sleepily peaceful, they gave themselves fully to God in prayer. His peace then stayed with them all day. The best time for prayer, concluded Catherine Marshall, isn't found; it's made.

Piecing the Pattern Together

I'll never forget the day my oldest son got his first job. I won't forget it because of what he spent his first paycheck on. At the age of 9, Zack bought himself a daily journal book. The next morning, while I was sitting quietly in my study, Zack tiptoed through the door with his brand new journal in one hand, and his devotional Bible in the other. Leaning his head on my shoulder and whispering in my ear, Zack asked, "Daddy, can you teach me how to have morning devotions?"

Somewhere along the line, Zack observed a pattern for time with God. As a result of observing the pattern, he decided he needed to find a pattern for himself. Holding back the tears in my eyes, I guided Zack through a simple pattern of devotions. Start with a short Bible reading, following that with prayer, and then writing a few notes about how the Lord spoke through the prayer and Bible reading time. Admittedly this is a simple pattern. However, it started him on his way to a wonderful piece of stained glass for what I hope and pray will be a life of seeking God through prayer.

With so many distractions, it's important one discovers a pattern for prayer which, in turn, helps keep a person focused on the task at hand. Of course, no pattern fits perfectly for everyone. After all, God has created us all to be individuals. However, we can learn from others. John Wesley recognized this important aspect of building a disciplined life of prayer. It is true, prayer, even though it should be the most natural part of our lives, is for most people the area of most struggle.

On the surface, most people blame time restraints for a

lack of prayer life. The line of thinking usually goes, "I'm just so busy, I don't have time for prayer." In the long run, discovering the right pattern usually presents the real issue of concern and difficulty. So just how does one piece a pattern together? Wesley knew the importance of pattern, and whenever anyone asked him for direction in prayer he'd send them straight to various written prayers beginning with the *Book of Common Prayer.* Why did he do this? Wesley understood well that the problem with prayer is how one approaches the whole area of prayer.

For centuries people have found themselves asking the same question as Zack — "Can you show me a pattern?" We should start our day and finish our day thinking on God. Having made a mental decision to do this, we must next discover the best time and the best way to spend time with the Lord. For some, it's as simple as the pattern laid out for Zack. For others, more time in reading may take place. For still others, more time may be spent in intercession for the concerns of friends and family. Some may spend a great deal of time listening for the voice of God if faced with an important decision, and still others may spend time mentally going through their daytimer asking for God's wisdom and guidance.

Whatever the case may be, pattern is important, because this is what helps a person focus on God and as a result put aside distractions of the day. Finding the perfect pattern will probably never happen. The reason for this revolves around the fact that life is constantly changing. Situations come and go just as seasons come and go. One season may bring heavy burdens for others. Another season may bring a time of listening and waiting on the Lord. But with a pattern pieced together, the changing seasons won't dim the stained glass.

In his book, *Preacher And Prayer,* later re-released under the title, *Power Through Prayer,* Methodist preacher E.M. Bounds

pointed out how prayer is not a petty duty placed in a corner only to
be pulled out when absolutely necessary. Prayer is not a performance
made out of fragments of time snatched from business and other en-
gagements of life. The best of our time, the heart of our time, and our
strength must be given to the important area of prayer in our life.
Prayer giving color and bent to our character should not be treated as
a hurried pastime. Praying is spiritual work. Human nature, of course,
does not like hard spiritual work. Bounds points out how human nature would rather sail to heaven under a favoring breeze and a full
smooth sea. However, prayer is work, because prayer requires discipline.

One of two things happens in the area of prayer. Either
people spend little time in prayer or no time at all. Of these two
problem areas, praying little may be worse than not praying at all.
Little praying creates a make-believe world in which a delusion of all
being well grows. Praying little becomes a bandaid for keeping spiritual cuts and bruises in place. Prayer requires discipline and pattern. It
is neither something pinned onto us as a reward for growing up, nor is
it something regulated to a mere 15 seconds of grace over an hour's
dinner. Prayer is serious work, taking years of practice and discipline
in order to discover a pattern that fits best to the individual.

Revisiting the Lord's Prayer

Why is the discipline of prayer one we should seek after?
In 1748, John Wesley preached a sermon providing an answer for such
a question.

Our Father

"*Our Father:* If he is a Father, then he is good, he is loving
to his children. And here is the first and great reason for prayer. God is

willing to bless; let us ask for a blessing.

"*Our Father:* Our Creator; the Author of our being; he who raised us from the dust of the earth; who breathed into us the breath of life, and we became living souls. But if he made us, let us ask, and he will not withhold any good thing from the work of his own hands.

"*Our Father:* Our Preserver who, day by day sustains the life he has given; of whose continuing love we now and every moment receive life and breath and all things. So much the more boldly let us come to him, and we shall obtain mercy and find grace to help in time of need. Above all, the Father of Our Lord Jesus Christ, and of all that believe in him; who justifies us freely by his grace, through the redemption that is in Jesus; who has blotted out all our sins, and healed all our infirmities; who has received us for his own children, by adoption and grace; and because we are sons and daughters, has sent forth the Spirit of his son into our hearts, crying, Abba, Father; who has given us second birth from seed not capable of rotting, and created us new in Christ Jesus. Therefore we know that he hears us always; therefore we pray to him without ceasing. We pray because we love; and we love him because he first loved us.

Forgiveness — As We Forgive
Those Who Trespass Against Us

"In these words our Lord clearly declares both on what condition, and in what degree or manner, we may expect to be forgiven by God. All our trespasses and sins are forgiven us, *if* we forgive others. This is a point of the utmost importance. Our blessed Lord is so concerned that we not let it slip out of our thoughts that he not only puts it in the body of the Lord's Prayer, but after the prayer repeats it. 'If,' he says, 'you forgive men their trespasses, your heavenly Father will also forgive you. But if you don't forgive others, your heavenly Father will not forgive you.'

"God forgives us as we forgive others. So that if any malice or bitterness, if any taint of unkindness or anger remains, if we do not clearly, fully and from the heart forgive everyone his or her sins, we so far cut short the forgiveness of God for us. God, then, cannot clearly and fully forgive us; he may show us some degree of mercy, but we do not allow him to blot out all our sins and forgive all our iniquities.

"If we do not, from our hearts, forgive our neighbor, what kind of prayer are we really offering to God when we say the Lord's Prayer?"

Lead Us Not Into Temptation

"The word translated *temptation* means trial of any kind. And so the English word 'temptation' was formerly taken in a general sense, though now it is usually understood as solicitation to sin. Saint James uses the word in both senses: first, in its general way, then in its more confined way. He takes it in the former sense when he says, 'Blessed is the man that endures temptation, for when he is tried, he shall receive the crown of life' (James 1:12). Then James uses the word in the more specific sense: 'Let no one say, when he is tempted, I am tempted of God. For God cannot be tempted with evil, neither can he tempt anyone. But every one is tempted when he is drawn by his or her own lust or desire' (James 1:13-14). James here talks about being enticed, caught as a fish with bait. Then he enters into temptation. Then temptation covers one like a cloud; it overspreads the whole soul. Then how hard it is to escape the snare! Therefore, we plead with God not to lead us into temptation; that is, not to let us be caught in it."

John Wesley — 1748
Upon Our Lord's Sermon On The Mount

Soldering the Pattern in Place

Working with stained glass not only takes time, but it also takes great care and patience. Once the pattern is drawn with the template in place, the glass is cut. Next the edges are ground and roughed in preparation for the attaching of the foil. The foil sticks to the glass only when the edges are rough. Once all the pieces are in place they're soldered together.

A life of prayer is very similar to piecing together stained glass. There are many patterns and templates, and the spiritual discipline of regular daily prayer time takes hard work and much grinding. The discipline of prayer is not an easy one that comes overnight. Only through the ups and downs of life will the discipline of prayer be allowed to stick to an individual's life. The soldering process of the various prayer pieces will never be complete as long as one remains open to the guidance of God. Prayer is a lifetime commitment of seeking the Lord with all your heart, soul and mind. When one seeks God in this fashion many pieces fall into place in the area of a personal devotion life.

Written forms of prayers can and will lead to a pattern for a consistent and productive prayer life. A pattern for devotion is a personal topic. However, once the frame is in place from a knowledge of various written prayers, the stained glass pattern begins taking shape for a life of prayer with relevance and meaning to where you currently live.

When first beginning ministry, the Lord allowed my path to cross with a faithful prayer warrior. Then a retired minister, he decided to pray for a new kid on the block. I enjoyed many hours of conversation with this praying saint, and only once did he ever allow me to pray for him. When I visited him in the hospital, the warrior knew his days on earth were coming to an end. At the close of our conversation, I asked if I could pray. Holding hands and bowing our heads, I asked the Lord to be near.

I don't think I'll ever forget what happened next, for a couple reasons. First, because of what he said, and second, because the next day he went home to be with the Lord. As a result, these were his last words of encouragement to me. After we finished praying I turned to leave, but he wouldn't let go of my hand.

With tear-filled eyes he grasped my hand with all the remaining strength in his body. This defender of the gospel said, "Rus, my friend and my brother, there's something I want you to always remember. Know this, I prayed for you daily during these last couple years, and I will continue praying for you in the years to come. The only difference will be instead of bowing here on earth, I'll be standing before the very throne of God asking for His grace, peace and mercy to be with you always.'"

This was a stained glass pattern for devotion, brought to perfection before the very throne of grace.

CHAPTER FIVE

Open Windows — Grace of Hearing

"Everyone who has this hope in him
purifies himself, just as he is pure."
1 John 3:3

With her husband, Edmund Gravely, dying at the controls of his small plane while flying to Statesboro, GA, from the Rocky Mount-Wilson airport, NC, Janice Gravely kept the plane aloft for two hours until it ran out of fuel. During this time she sang hymns and prayed for help. As the plane crossed the South Carolina-North Carolina border she radioed for help saying, "Help, help! Won't someone help me? My pilot is unconscious. Won't somebody please help me?"

Authorities who picked up her distress signal were unable to reach her by radio during the flight, because she kept changing channels. Mrs. Gravely finally made a crash landing and crawled for 45 minutes to a farmhouse in search of help. Had she not kept changing channels, those hearing the distress call might have been able to help her land the plane safely on an airstrip.

Many times God's people cry out for help and then switch channels before His message comes through. People turn to other sources for help, usually looking for human help. When crying out to God for His intervention, don't switch channels before He has a chance to answer. When channels are switched, you risk losing out on hearing a wonderful message.

How can one recognize the still small voice of God? "Only when one has a patterned life of devotion seeking the heart and will of God." As one grows nearer to God through the avenue of prayer, it becomes easier to distinguish God's voice from others calling for attention.

A patterned devotional life results in relevant prayers in which a person not only prays but also listens. No longer does a person simply pray, "Our Father." Instead, he prays, "My Father, who art in heaven."

With the stained glass pieces in place, one's prayer life becomes relevant to where the worshiper is living, as opposed to prayers merely representing words on a page. The artist, having spent hours piecing together the window, finds himself admiring the work and knowing firsthand the blood, sweat and tears it took to create it in the first place.

With the pattern in place, worshipers begin focusing not on *how* to pray, but rather *to Whom* they are praying. With this changed attitude, one becomes aware of the fact that prayer is not simply a one-sided task. With the window of grace now open, the grace of hearing kicks in, and one can hear God speaking, encouraging the worshiper to grow deeper in relationship with Him.

Pattern Leading to Personal Experience

Can a person truly find the heart of God once a pattern is in place? This is like asking: Can a person become a good cook by cooking much? The answer to both questions is yes. John Wesley established a pattern of devotion long before his personal experience with the Lord. Through the established daily pattern of prayer, Wesley soon found himself drawing nearer to God and as a result able to recognize His voice. You could say Wesley's pattern led to a personal experience.

One of the most often quoted Wesley journal entries is his "heart-warming experience" that occurred at Aldersgate on May 24, 1738. Many times, however, a large portion of his entry for that day is either left out or totally ignored. Yes, the actual experience is important, but we must be careful not to ignore the complete process that ultimately led Wesley to his experience with Christ. In the process described by John Wesley himself, we discover how the pattern did lead to experience.

Monday, Tuesday and Wednesday:

"I had continual sorrow and heaviness in my heart: Something of which I described, in the broken manner I was able, in the following letter to a friend: —

"O why is it, that so great, so wise, so holy a God will use such an instrument as me! Lord, 'let the dead bury their dead!' But will you send the dead to raise the dead? I see that the whole law of God is holy, just and good. I know every thought, every temper of my soul ought to bear God's image and superscription. But how am I fallen from the glory of God! I feel that I am sold under sin. I know that I too deserve nothing but wrath, being full of all abominations: And having no good thing in me to atone for them, or to remove the wrath of God. All my works, my righteousness, my prayers, need an atonement for themselves. So that my mouth is stopped. I have nothing to plead. God is holy, I am unholy. God is a consuming fire: I am altogether a sinner.

"Yet I hear a voice (and is it not the voice of God?) saying 'Believe and you shall be saved. He that believes has passed from death unto life. God so loved the world that He gave His only Son, that whoever believes in Him should not perish, but have everlasting life.'

"O let no one deceive us by vain words. By its fruits we shall know. Do we already feel peace with God, and joy in the Holy Ghost? Does His Spirit bear witness with our spirit, that we are the children of God? Alas, with mine He does not. O Saviour of men, save us from trusting in anything but You! Draw us after You! Let us be emptied ourselves, and then fill us with all peace and joy in believing, and let nothing separate us from your love in time or in eternity.

"What occurred on *Wednesday, 24*, I think best to relate at large, after premising what may make it the better understood. Let him that cannot receive it ask of the Father of lights, that He would give more light to him and me.

"I believe, till I was about ten years old I had not sinned away that 'washing of the Holy Ghost' which was given me in baptism; having been strictly educated and carefully taught, that I could only be saved 'by universal obedience, by keeping all the commandments of God'; in the meaning of which I was diligently instructed. Those instructions, so far as they respected outward duties and sins, I gladly received, and often thought of. But all that was said to me of inward obedience, or holiness, I neither understood nor remembered. So that I was indeed as ignorant of the true meaning of the Law, as I was of the Gospel of Christ.

"The next six or seven years were spent at school; where, outward restraints being removed, I was much more negligent than before, even of outward duties, and almost continually guilty of outward sins, which I knew to be such, though they were not scandalous in the eye of the world. However, I still read the Scriptures, and said my prayers, morning and evening. And what I now hoped to be saved by, was, 1. Not being so bad as other people. 2. Having still a kindness for religion. And, 3. Reading the Bible, going to church, and saying my prayers.

"Being removed to the University for five years, I still said my prayers both in public and in private, and read, with the Scriptures, several other books of religion, especially comments on the New Testament. Yet I had not all this while so much as a notion of inward holiness; nay, went on habitually, and, for the most part, very contentedly, in some or other known sin.

"When I was about twenty-two, my father pressed me to enter into holy orders. At the same time, the providence of God directing me to Thomas à Kempis' *Christian Pattern,* I began to see, that true religion was seated in the heart, and that God's law extended to all our thoughts as well as words and actions. I set apart an hour or two a day for religious retirement. I communicated [attended worship] every week. I began to aim at, and pray for, inward holiness. So that now, doing so much, and living so good a life, I doubted not but I was a good Christian.

"I began to see more and more the value of time. I applied myself closer to study. I advised others to be religious, according to that scheme of religion by which I modeled my own life. But meeting now with Mr. Law's *Christian Perfection* and *Serious Call,* although I was much offended at many parts of both, yet they convinced me more than ever of the exceeding height and breadth and depth of the law of God.

"In 1730 I began visiting the prisons; assisting the poor and sick in town; and doing what other good I could, by my presence, or my little fortune, to the bodies and souls of all men. Yet, when after continuing some years in this course, I apprehended myself to be near death, I could not find that all this gave me any comfort, or any assurance of acceptance with God. At this I was then not a little surprised; not imagining I had been all this time building on the sand, nor con-

sidering that 'other foundation can no man lay, than that which is laid'
by God, 'even Christ Jesus.'

"Soon after, a contemplative man convinced me still more
than I was convinced before, that outward works are nothing, being
alone; and in several conversations instructed me, how to pursue inward holiness, or a union of the soul with God. During this whole
struggle between nature and grace, which had now continued above
ten years, I had many remarkable returns to prayer; especially when I
was in trouble.

"In my return to England, January 1738, being in imminent
danger of death, and very uneasy on that account, I was strongly
convinced that the cause of that uneasiness was unbelief; and that the
gaining a true, living faith was the one thing needful for me.

"When I met Peter Bohler, he consented to put the dispute
upon the issue which I desired, namely, Scripture and experience. I
first consulted the Scripture. But when I set aside the glosses of men,
and simply considered the words of God, comparing them together,
endeavouring to illustrate the obscure by the plainer passages; I found
they all made against me, and was forced to retreat to my last hold,
'that experience would never agree with the literal interpretation of
those scriptures. Nor could I therefore allow it to be true, till I found
some living witnesses of it.' He replied, he could show me such at any
time. The next day he came again with three others, all of whom
testified, of their own personal experience, that a true living faith in
Christ is inseparable from a sense of pardon for all past, and freedom
from all present sins. They added with one mouth, that this faith was
the gift, the free gift of God, and that He would surely bestow it upon
every soul who earnestly and perseveringly sought it.

"I was now thoroughly convinced, and by the grace of
God, I resolved to seek it unto the end, 1. By absolutely renouncing all

dependence, in whole or in part, upon *my own* works or righteousness; on which I had really grounded my hope of salvation, though I knew it not from my youth up. 2. By adding to the constant use of all the other means of grace, continual prayer for this very thing, justifying, saving faith, a full reliance on the blood of Christ shed for *me;* a trust in Him, as *my* Christ, as *my* sole justification, sanctification, and redemption.

"I continued thus to seek it till Wednesday, May 24. I think it was about five this morning, that I opened my Testament on those words, 'There are given to us exceeding great and precious promises, even that you should be partakers of the divine nature' (2 Peter 1:4). Just as I went out, I opened it again on those words, 'You are not far from the kingdom of God.'

"In the evening I went very unwillingly to a society in Aldersgate-Street, where one was reading Luther's preface to the Epistle to the Romans. About a quarter before nine, while he was describing the change which God works in the heart through faith in Christ, I felt my heart strangely warmed. I felt I did trust in Christ, Christ alone for salvation. An assurance was given me, that He had taken away *my* sins, even *mine*, and saved *me* from the law of sin and death. I then testified openly to all there, what I now first felt in my heart.

"After my return home, I was much buffeted with temptations; but cried out, and they fled away. They returned again and again. I as often lifted up my eyes, and He 'sent help from His holy place.' Herein I found the difference between this and my former state chiefly consisted. I was striving, yes, fighting with my might under the law, as well as under grace. But then I was sometimes, if not often, conquered. Now, I was always conqueror.

"*Thursday, 25* — The moment I awaked, 'Jesus, Master,' was in my heart and in my mouth, and I found all my strength lay in keeping my eye fixed upon Him, and my soul waiting on Him continually. Being again at St. Paul's in the afternoon, I could taste the good word of God in the anthem, which began, 'My song shall be always of the loving kindness of the Lord: With my mouth will I ever be showing forth your truth from one generation to another.'"

John Wesley Journal — May 1738

A patterned life of devotion, put into place years prior, first by the training of his mother, then developed while in school, eventually placed John Wesley face to face with the risen Lord. A pattern of devotion led to a personal experience of accepting Jesus into his heart. A pattern of devotion not only enabled him to recognize and hear the voice of God, but it also helped him pray for help and guidance when "buffeted with temptations."

Holding onto the Line

A woman once telephoned the manager of a large opera house and told him she had lost a valuable diamond pin the night before at a concert. The man asked her to hold the line for a moment while he looked. A search was made, and the brooch was found. However, when the manager got back to the phone, the woman had hung up. He waited for her to call again, and even put a notice in the newspaper concerning the found diamond pin. He heard nothing further from the woman.

What a strange and foolish person we say to ourselves, but isn't this the way some people pray as well? We tell the Lord all about our needs and then don't stay on the line long enough to hear His answers. As a result, we miss the joy of answered prayer and the thrill and reward of a persistent faith.

With a pattern for prayer in place, and a heart seeking God, the lines of communication are opened in two directions. Not only does the Lord hear our prayers, but He also answers them. As one spends more and more time with God, it in turn becomes easier to hear His voice. Of course, as soon as we say this, someone is always quick to point out that they never know when God answers their prayers. One of the barriers to answered prayer is as simple as not writing them down.

Many people pray many things. However, few actually keep track of what they're praying for. Another important aspect of the pattern for prayer and devotion is the keeping of a prayer journal. This does not have to be an elaborate tracking method. Use whatever works best for you. In my case, I have a simple spiral note pad. On one side I jot down requests, and on the opposite page I write in answers to prayer. A quick deterrent for prayer is the feeling none are answered. A great encouragement for prayer is knowing God answers prayer as one keeps track of various prayer requests throughout the weeks and months.

How did John Wesley know God answered prayer? He knew, because he kept track of answered prayers in his journal.

"I was desired to preach at Thame, on my return to London. I arrived a little after ten. The mob had been so troublesome there, that it was a doubt with the Preachers, whether the place should not be given up. I went into a large building and it was quickly filled, and more than filled, many stood outside. There was no breath of noise. We had prayed before, that God would give us a quiet time, and He granted us our request.

"Immediately after, a strange scene occurred. I was desired to visit one who had been eminently pious, but had now been confined to her bed for several months, and was utterly unable to raise herself up. She desired us to pray, that the chain might be broken. A few of us prayed in faith. Presently she rose up, dressed herself, came down stairs and I believe had not any farther complaint."

John Wesley Journal — Oct. 16, 1778

Wesley also collected other people's accounts of the grace of hearing. One such collection appears as an entry in his journal from 1782.

"I had now leisure to transcribe a letter, wrote last May, from Amherst, in Nova Scotia, by a young man.

"In the year 1779, I saw, if I would go to heaven, I must lead a new life. But I did not know I wanted an inward change till I was at a prayer-meeting held at Mr. Oxley's. While they were praying, my heart began to throb within me, my eyes gushed out with tears, and I cried aloud for mercy. In a few moments, it pleased God to fill Mrs. Oxley with joy unspeakable. After this, we went, almost every night, to Mr. Oxley's to sing and pray. A few weeks later, an old Methodist, after praying with me said, 'I think you will get the blessing before morning.' About two hours after, while we were singing a hymn, it pleased God to reveal his Son in my heart. Since that time, I have had many blessed days, and many happy nights.

"One Sunday night, after my brother Dicky and I were gone to bed, I asked him, 'Can you believe?' He answered, 'No.' I exhorted him to wrestle hard with God, and got up to pray with him. But he was unbelieving still: So I went to sleep again. Yet, not being satisfied, after talking largely to him, I got up again, and began praying for him; being fully persuaded that God would set his soul at liberty. And so he did: He pardoned all his sins, and bade him 'go in peace.'

"It being now between twelve and one, I waked my brothers, John and Thomas, and told them the glad tidings. They got up. We went to prayer; and when we rose from our knees, Tommy declared, 'God has blotted out all my sins.' I then went to my father and mother, (who were both seeking salvation,) and told them the joyful news. My father said, 'Willy, pray for us.' I did, and earnestly exhorted him to wrestle with God for himself. So he did, and it was not long before God set his soul also at liberty. These are a few of the wonderful works of God among us: But he is also working on the hearts of the inhabitants in general."

John Wesley Journal — April 15, 1782

In 1790 Wesley writes of a miracle as a direct answer to prayer.

"Here an eminently pious woman, Mrs. Jones, at whose house I stopped, gave me a very strange account: — Many years since she was much hurt in lying-in. She had various Physicians, but still grew worse and worse, till, perceiving herself to be no better, she left them off. She had continual pain, and was soon confined to her bed. There she lay two months, helpless and hopeless, till a thought came to her mind, 'Lord, if you will, you can make me whole! Be it according to your will!' Immediately the pain and the disorder ceased. Feeling herself well, she rose, and dressed herself. Her husband coming in, and seeing her in tears, asked, 'Are those tears of sorrow or joy?' She said, 'Of joy!' on which they wept together. From that hour she felt no pain, but enjoyed perfect health. I think our Lord never wrought a plainer miracle."

John Wesley Journal — Oct. 7, 1790

What do these accounts tell us? They reveal the grace of hearing through answered prayer. Time and time again God answers prayer, and when one keeps track of the requests, the grace of hearing becomes real and alive because answered prayer is God speaking.

Answered Prayer — Grace of Hearing

I read of a Christian businessman who experienced a call into full-time ministry. Selling his business at a loss, he went into Christian ministry, where things became somewhat rough. There were four children in the family, and one night during a time of family devotions, Timmy, the youngest boy, asked, "Daddy, do you think Jesus would mind if I asked Him for a shirt?"

"Well of course not," replied his father, "let's write that down in our prayer request book."

His mother wrote down "shirt for Timmy," and she added "size seven." Timmy, of course, knowing his request was written down, made sure the family prayed for his shirt every day. After a number of weeks the mother received a telephone call from a local store owner.

"I've just finished my July clearance sale and, knowing you have four boys, it occurred to me that you might be able to use something of what we have left. Could you use some boy's shirts?"

She asked, "What size?"

"Size seven," replied the businessman.

"How many do you have?" she asked somewhat hesitantly.

"Twelve."

Many of us might have taken those shirts, stuffed them into a dresser drawer, and made a casual comment to the child. Not this set of parents. That night, just as expected, Timmy said, "Don't forget, Mommy and Daddy, we need to pray for a shirt."

"We don't have to pray for the shirt tonight, Timmy," responded the mother.

"How come?"

"The Lord has answered your prayer."

"He has?"

Then, just as planned, Timmy's brother Tommy went out and got one of the shirts and placed it on the table. Little Timmy's eyes were like saucers. Tommy went back out, retrieving another shirt, and brought it back in as well. Out and back, out and back, out and back, until finally there were 12 shirts neatly piled on the table in front of Timmy. By this point, Timmy thought God had gone into the shirt business.

The grace of hearing. When one truly seeks the Lord through prayer on a daily and regular basis, the lines of communication, the wonderful window of grace, is opened and ready for two-way communication. Many people miss the grace of hearing either from changing channels too quickly or simply not keeping track of prayer requests. Once a person begins the pattern of praying, writing and listening, the pattern of devotion becomes a life-long process. Once we hear the still small voice of God, it's an experience we want to continue forever.

Somewhere today there's a boy named Timothy who's probably establishing his own pattern of devotion. Why? Because he believes there's a God in heaven who's interested enough in his needs to provide a little boy with shirts.

Window Maintenance — A Life of Prayer

"Therefore, I urge you, brothers, in view of God's
mercy, to offer your bodies as living sacrifices,
holy and pleasing to God — this is your spiritual act
of worship. Do not conform any longer to the
pattern of this world, but be transformed by the
renewing of your mind. Then you will be able
to test and approve what God's will is — His good,
pleasing, and perfect will."
Romans 12:1-2

C. H. Spurgeon once described prayer as pulling the rope down below and ringing the bells above in the ears of God. Some hardly stir the bell, because they pray so weakly, while others give only an occasional jerk at the rope. The person who truly communicates with God in heaven is the one who grasps the rope boldly and pulls continuously with all his might.

Once the window of grace is opened, from time to time window maintenance is required. As we offer ourselves continually to God, we need to know prayer has its ebbs and flows. As one grasps the rope boldly, there's a need to understand and know that prayer is not just a method to be learned. It is a life to be lived. With that in mind it's now time to explore the important area of maintaining a life of prayer. Sure killers of prayer are hardships discovered in maintaining a consistent prayer life. Just because the proper steps have been followed doesn't necessarily mean a rich prayer life will follow at all times.

Don't forget that for many years before John Wesley's heart-warming experience, he himself prayed often. Much of the disciplined methodical approach to a devout and holy life came before his 1738 experience. But even through the methodical prayer, he always felt he was missing out on something of the heart of God. Prayer comes to life once persons have experienced the heart-warming presence of the Lord in their lives. Then, the great window of grace, known as prayer, takes on new life. The new vitality leads to a life truly seeking God's will.

Prayer Through Pattern and Method

Some may wonder if the only people who understand method are the Methodists. Does one have to be a Methodist in the Wesleyan tradition to fully understand prayer through pattern and method? Of course not! Prayer is the most natural thing a person can do. Many distractions take our eyes off the importance of prayer, but the bottom line is that humankind was created to have fellowship with God. As a result, prayer should be natural. In many cases, it's not because of the fact that it's a discipline to be learned and a life to be lived. Maintaining a life of prayer is hard work.

Does one have to be a Methodist to have a corner on prayer? No. Did John Wesley invent his methodical approach to a disciplined life of seeking the Lord with all his heart, soul and mind? No. So then, what exactly is a *Methodist?* Interestingly enough, this question has actually been around for years.

In his *Short History of Methodism,* Wesley wrote:

"In November, 1729, four young gentlemen of Oxford — Mr. John Wesley, Fellow of Lincoln College; Mr. Charles Wesley, Student of Christ Church; Mr. Morgan, Commoner of Christ Church; and Mr. Kirkham, of Merton College, — began to spend some evenings in a week together, in reading, chiefly, the Greek Testament. The next year two or three of Mr. John Wesley's pupils desired the liberty of meeting with them; and afterwards one of Mr. Charles Wesley's pupils. It was in 1732, that Mr. Ingham, of Queen's College, and Mr. Broughton, of Exeter, were added to their number. To these, in April, was joined Mr. Clayton, of Brazen-nose, with two or three of his pupils. About the same time Mr. James Hervey was permitted to meet with them; and in 1735, Mr. Whitefield.

"The exact regularity of their lives, as well as studies, occasioned a young gentleman of Christ Church to say, 'Here is a new set of Methodists sprung up.' The name was new and quaint, so it took immediately, and the Methodists were known all over the University."

Wesley wrote, "Since the name first came into the world, many have been at a loss to know what a Methodist is. What are the principles and the practice of those who are commonly called by that name? What are the distinguishing marks of this group?

"I say those who are called Methodists, and let it be well observed that this is not a name which they take to themselves, but one fixed on them by others. I should rejoice if the very name might never be mentioned, but be buried in eternal oblivion. But if that cannot be, at least let those who will use it, know the meaning of the word they use. Let us not always be fighting in the dark. Come, and let us look one another in the face. Perhaps some of you who hate what I am *called,* may love what I *am* by the grace of God. Or rather, what I follow after.

"The distinguishing marks of a Methodist are not his opinions of any sort. His assenting to this or that scheme of religion, his embracing any particular set of notions, his espousing the judgment of one man or of another, are quite wide of the point. Whosoever, therefore, imagines that a Methodist is a man of such or such an opinion, is grossly ignorant of the whole affair. He mistakes the truth totally.

"Nor do we desire to be distinguished by actions, customs, or usage's, of an indifferent nature. Our religion does not lie in doing what God has not enjoined, or abstaining from what He has not forbidden. It does not lie in the form of our apparel, in the posture of our body, or the covering of our heads. Nor in abstaining from marriage, or from meats and drinks, which are all good if received with thanksgiving. Therefore, neither will any man, who knows what he affirms, fix the mark of a Methodist here.

"Nor, lastly, is he distinguished by laying the whole stress of religion on any single part of it. If you say, 'Yes, he is, for he thinks we are saved by faith alone.' I answer, 'You do not understand the terms.' By salvation he means holiness of heart and life. We know by experience a man may labor many years, and at the end have no religion at all, no more than he had at the beginning.

"What then is the mark? Who is a Methodist, according to your own account? I answer: A Methodist is one who has the love of God in his heart. A Methodist is one who loves the Lord his God with all his heart, and with all his soul, and with all his mind, and with all his strength. God is the joy of his heart, and the desire of his soul.

"A Methodist is one who 'prays without ceasing.' It is given him 'always to pray, and not to faint.' Not that he is always in the house of prayer, though he neglects no opportunity of being there. Neither is he always on his knees, although he often is, or on his face, before the Lord his God. Nor yet is he always crying aloud to God, or calling upon him in words. For many times 'the Spirit makes intercession for him.' His heart is ever lifted up to God, at all times and in all places. In this he is never hindered, much less interrupted, by any person or thing. In retirement or company, in leisure, business, or conversation, his heart is ever with the Lord. Whether he lie down or rise up, God is in all his thoughts. He walks with God continually, having the loving eye of his mind still fixed upon him, and everywhere 'seeing Him that is invisible.'

"Agreeable to this his one desire, is the one design of his life, namely, 'not to do his will, but the will of Him that sent him.' His one intention at all times and in all things is, not to please himself, but Him whom his soul loves. He has a single eye, and because his eye is single, his whole body is full of light. Where the loving eye of the soul is continually fixed on God, there can be no darkness at all. God reigns alone. All that is in the soul is holiness to the Lord. There is not a motion in his heart, but is according to his will. Every thought that arises points to Him, and is in obedience to the law of Christ."

John Wesley, *Character of a Methodist* — 1742

Christianity 101

I've recently discovered an interest in church history. With this interest comes the realization that the most important aspect of any denomination or sect must be centered on discovering the will of God. One day, in a church history class at seminary, the discussion turned to B.T. Roberts, the founder of the Free Methodist Church in 1860. The professor was not speaking very kindly of Roberts. I quickly interjected how the formation of the Free Methodist Church came out of a concern for communicating the gospel to all people. Somewhere along the line, the Methodist church had lost sight of this goal.

If, I reasoned with the professor, you consider B.T. Roberts as a church breaker, you must also consider the founding fathers of the Methodist church in the same light. John Wesley never intended for the Methodist movement to become a denomination. He always dreamed of the day when the Anglicans, under the umbrella of which he worked, would turn their *hearts* toward God. To put it plain and simple — Methodism is Christianity 101.

"These are the principles and practices of our sect. These are the marks of a true Methodist. By these alone do those who are in derision so called, desire to be distinguished from other men. If any man say, 'Why, these are only the common fundamental principles of Christianity!' You are right! I know they are no other, and I pray to God that you, and all men recognized this fact. I, and all who follow my judgment, do vehemently refuse to be distinguished from other men, by any but the common principles of Christianity. The plain old Christianity I teach, renouncing and detesting all other marks of distinction. And whosoever is what I preach, (let him be called what he will, for names change not the nature of things,) he is a Christian, not in name only, but in heart and life. He is inwardly and outwardly conformed to the will of God, as revealed in the written Word. He thinks, speaks, and lives, according to the method laid down in the revelation of Jesus Christ. His soul is renewed after the image of God, in righteousness, and in all true holiness. And having the mind that was in Christ, he so walks as Christ also walked."

John Wesley, *Character of a Methodist* — 1742

Maintaining a patterned life of prayer has nothing to do with being a Free Methodist, Methodist, Wesleyan or whatever other denominational tag you might want to hang on it. Maintaining a life of prayer and keeping the wonderful window of grace open revolves around seeking the heart of God. The words of Paul from Romans 12 call all Christians to be patterned after God, not the world. This also was one of John Wesley's favorite passages. Expanding on these verses, Wesley encouraged people to live holy lives.

"You are called to show by the whole tenor of your life and conversation that you are 'renewed in the spirit of your mind, after the image of Him that created you: and that your rule is ... the good and acceptable and perfect will of God."

John Wesley, Sermon LXXX — *"On Friendship with the World"*

No One Said It Would Be Easy

Is a life of prayer an easy one? Put quite simply, no. With window maintenance maintaining a life of prayer, can one find happiness and peace with God? Yes, but no one said it would be easy. I remember one medication I hated taking when I was a kid. I knew in the end it would help, but I never wanted to take it. When things weren't moving quite right, Mom would give my brothers and me a spoonful of castor oil. Thinking about it now brings back memories of the oily coating left behind in my mouth after that spoonful of medicine went down. Nothing tasted quite right for about an hour. We never liked taking the castor oil, but we knew it was good for us, no matter how distasteful it was.

Discipline is always a hard pill to swallow. However, with a pattern in place, the disciplined habit of prayer helps smooth over rough spots in life. Sometimes when people recognize *why* they struggle, the solution, discipline, becomes easier. An amazing aspect of life involves the idea that when the going gets tough, often the first thing to go is a relationship with God. Many people instantly say, "If this happens to me as I believe and pray, why bother believing or praying?"

In a world of instant fixes, prayer sometimes fights a losing battle, because in many cases it's not an instant fix. Abortion on demand instantly fixes that unwanted pregnancy. Plea bargaining takes care of the stiffer sentence in the area of crimes committed, and, if you have a good lawyer, you may even get off totally free! If you don't like the way your face looks, call a plastic surgeon and get a face lift. Tired of your spouse? Call up a lawyer and file for divorce. We live in a world that seems like it can almost instantly fix anything. However, the quick fix never lasts. Somewhere along the line life becomes a stream of quick fixes that never totally take care of the real problem.

Maintenance from the Right Place

I have a confession to make. I'm not a mechanic. Just ask my mechanic; he'll tell you. I can do little things like check the oil and radiator level, but when a real problem arises, off to the mechanic I go. One day, I noticed my car was running a little roughly. I quickly headed for the garage. Looking under the hood, we decided an oil change was needed and possibly new spark plugs. With the work completed, I took off for a day of running around. The car got worse. Not only was it running roughly, but it was also puffing a lot of white smoke on start-up. Back at the garage, we decided fuel injector cleaner in the gas tank would cure the ailments of my poor little Honda.

The next day, I left the Honda with my wife and took off in the van. Much to my dismay, upon arrival back home, the Honda wasn't in the driveway. My wife informed me it was still parked at our kid's school where it refused to start. After a few starting attempts, this time I towed it to the garage. When the mechanic looked under the hood, he discovered oil in the radiator overflow container. I knew I was in trouble. A week later, I had new head gaskets, and the head itself had been machined flat once again. I had no idea what was wrong with the car. Through step by step maintenance, however, my mechanic discovered that the problem was a warped engine head. Once the problem was identified, he fixed it.

One's spiritual life is like that, too. Many times people wait until the last possible moment before calling out to God. When life hits rock bottom, people finally call out praying, "Dear Lord, get me out of this jam, and I promise I'll never bother You again!" The sad reality is, in most cases people never do turn to the Lord again. What a shame. God is much more than a "fix-it man" you call as a last possible resource. God is Someone Who's always waiting for His children to spend time with Him in prayer.

Method and pattern establish a lasting relationship. With the pattern in place, the hard times become somewhat easier to overcome, because you know the source of help. Maintaining a disciplined life of prayer helps identify that still small voice when He speaks to you. When faced with difficult decisions and conflicting voices in your mind, when a life of prayer is in place, the Lord helps you find His peace while sorting through the confusion.

The Benefits of Pattern

Among the benefits that come to those who continue steadfastly in prayer is the joy of having God draw near to you. This thought is captured in an interesting poem by Perry Tanksley entitled *"The Visitor."* The poem gives a brief but stirring biography of a humble Christian by the name of Jim.

> For years each day at six a.m.
> He went to church and bowed his knee
> And meekly prayed, "Dear God, it's Jim,"

And when he'd leave, we all could see
The Presence came and walked with him.

As Jim grew old, the chastening rod
Of years left him so ill and drawn
His path to church is now untrod,
But in his room each day at dawn,
He hears a voice, "Dear Jim, it's God."

Perry Tanksley

© Used By Permission

It takes effort and preparation to pray meaningfully. It takes diligence to pray faithfully. Yet prayer is not a burden, but a glorious opportunity that in turn brings rich rewards.

John Wesley lived, worked, taught and breathed a highly-disciplined life of prayer. His methodical approach to God, seeking Him with all his heart, soul, mind and strength, rewarded him well. In the good times, he praised the Lord, and in the hard times he praised the Lord even louder. Until the end, he was full of praise, counsel and words of encouragement. In his last moments, with what remaining strength he had, John Wesley cried out twice in a voice of triumph, "The best of all is, God is with us!" The last word Wesley was heard to articulate was, "Farewell!"

John Wesley, driven by an unquenchable thirst for inward holiness, knew the only way to God was on his knees. Prayer was not just an obligation for Wesley. Prayer was a way of life.

A Window of Grace

Part Two

CHAPTER SEVEN

Sixty Days with Wesley

Quiet time with God is a discipline, a discipline that must be made, and a discipline that is, even at different times in life, harder or easier for some. No one said a life of following the Lord, actively seeking His face each day, was an easy one. Life is full of adventures which at times turn into struggles. However, when we recognize why we struggle, then the solution — discipline — becomes easier.

John Wesley lived a disciplined life for some 60 years. We know it didn't come easy. Most people have no idea where to start in a disciplined devotional life. As a result, many feel terrified, overwhelmed and defeated before beginning. We tend to hold up the great prayer warriors as examples of how all people should pray, overlooking the fact that not all are called to such high levels of continuous time in prayer. This is not an excuse for the lack of a devotional life, though. All Christians are called to spend time with the Lord in prayer.

Some say there's no room in their daily timetable for prayer. Their lives are so busy with driving to work, taking care of the house and yard, walking the dog, and running the kids to after-school sports, that they think there's no time left for God. As a result of hectic lifestyles, time with the Lord disappears. Of course, some will say it was easy for people like John Wesley to pray all the time. He wasn't as busy as we are now. Life back then was much more laid back and slower.

This may be true to a certain extent, but this does not mean

John Wesley lived an unhurried life. He traveled some 250,000 miles in his lifetime. This was long before high speed jet travel, too! These miles were traveled either by foot or on horseback, and the average speed of a horse is somewhere around 5 mph. Not only did he travel, but Wesley also preached 40,000 to 45,000 sermons in his lifetime. So you see, John Wesley, this great man of prayer, did not live a boring and unhurried life.

Even with all the miles traveled and all the sermons preached, John Wesley never lost touch with his quiet time before the Lord. How long did he actually spend in prayer? It all depends on how you count it. Wesley observed morning and evening prayer as outlined in the *Anglican Book of Common Prayer*. To these he added fixed times, times of personal prayer and meditation, as well as several minutes each hour to examine his spiritual temperament. An approximate day's average of two to three hours probably would not be excessive. Before you become overwhelmed saying I could never do that, remember that John Wesley was also just like the rest of us living today. Each day's demands expanded or contracted the time he spent in prayer.

Throughout his life, however, one thing did not change — Wesley's attitude concerning prayer and devotion. From his diaries and journals we discover he prayed often throughout the day. He prayed before each engagement and while writing letters. He also prayed with his soul friends and other small groups. He was in a state of meditation as he read the Scriptures or other materials as well. Last, but not least, he was in a state of prayer as he used the questions for self-examination at the beginning and ending of each day. You could say John Wesley didn't really have a devotional *time*. He had a devotional *life*.

How did Wesley maintain such a disciplined devotional

life? The answer revolves around his method. His methodical disciplined devotional life kept him in constant conversation with God at all times. Just who is a *Methodist?* According to Wesley, those who seek God with all their heart, soul and mind.

"It may be needful to specify whom I mean by this ambiguous term. Since it would be lost labor to speak to Methodists, so called, without first describing those to whom I speak.

"By Methodists I mean, a people who profess to pursue (in whatsoever measure they have attained) holiness of heart and life, inward and outward conformity in all things to the revealed will of God. Who place religion in a uniform resemblance of the great object of it, in a steady imitation of Him they worship, in all his imitable perfection's [sic]. More particularly, in justice, mercy, and truth, or universal love filling the heart, and governing the life.

"If you walk by this rule, continually endeavoring to know and love and resemble and obey the great God and Father of our Lord Jesus, as the God of love, of pardoning mercy. If from this principle of loving, obedient faith, you carefully abstain from all evil, and labour, as you have opportunity to do good to all men, friends or enemies; if, lastly, you unite together, to encourage and help each other in thus working out your salvation, and for that end watch over one another in love, you are they whom I mean by Methodists."

John Wesley — October 10, 1745

Advice to the People Called Methodists

You could say the method helps open the great window of grace leading to the throne room of God. The example of pattern is not a new concept or phenomenon concerning prayer. People have been writing about pattern for many years. Jesus gave a pattern to His disciples with the Lord's Prayer. Whenever a person asked John Wesley for guidance in prayer, he sent them straight to patterns. The challenge I lay before you now is to pray the pattern as outlined by Wesley many years ago. Wesley established his disciplined prayer life and stuck with it for 60 years. I now encourage you to try his pattern for 60 days.

At first, this may seem a little odd, and the content of the prayers may not perfectly fit our current situation. However, once people stay with the form for 60 days, the pattern becomes part of their lives. With the frame in place, and the stained glass pattern present, they are now ready for a life of prayer relevant to their own situation. Once the pattern is in place, the discipline aspect becomes secondary, and a joy of looking forward to meeting God enters.

To seek God with all of one's heart, soul and mind is not only a mandate for people called Methodists, but it's the mandate of every Christian living for Jesus. It's said of John Wesley that only eternity will reveal what the world owes to his ministry. He was active in ministry and prayer right up until the last. He was always full of praise, counsel and encouragement for others. Just before he died, he cried out in a voice of victory over death, "The best of all is, God is with us."

The founder of the movement known as Methodism, which is really a group of people seeking the Lord with all their strength, left a world of well traveled roads and musty pulpits to enter into the joy of the Lord for eternity. He called many people to the Lord by first calling them to their knees.

CHAPTER EIGHT

"Let the Adventure Begin"

Sorting through all of John Wesley's prayers proved both overwhelming and a blessing at the same time. John Wesley devoted not only much of his life to prayer, but also many written pages of prayers. What's known as the *Christian Library* contains the complete collection of his prayers for every day of the week. Since his death, others have pulled together samplings of Wesley's prayers. Some collections are quite short, and in some cases incomplete, because they don't truly capture Wesley's spirit of prayer. I in no way believe the collection of prayers found here will become a definitive collection, because Wesley himself already published those.

In the following pages I've endeavored to accomplish two things. First, I've attempted to give as complete a collection of the prayers as I can, without cutting too much out. Of course, some will say I've included too much, while others will say I've taken too much artistic liberty. One aspect of the prayers maintained here includes the opening words of adoration to God. These are very important, for one cannot approach God unless he first gives the Creator of life the worship, praise and adoration He deserves.

Secondly, I've tried updating the language so the prayers themselves are more timely for the age in which we live today. While spending time with the original forms of these prayers, I quickly discovered John Wesley prayed about issues of the day. Throughout the book, we've been looking at Wesley as a man providing a pattern for our window. Now, as I invite you to spend 60 days with Wesley, it makes sense to make his prayers relate to the world in which we live. This, of course, is something Wesley himself would have done as well.

Before sending you on this wonderful adventure of prayer, I also need to say that it's generally known that John Wesley made no bones over the fact that he made wholesale revisions of another person's work. In the preface of the *Christian Library,* he confessed quite frankly, "I have been obliged not only to omit … but also to add what was needful; either to clear their sense or to correct their mistakes. And in a design of this nature, I apprehend myself to be at full liberty to do so. I therefore take no author for better or worse."

Some wince at his method, and I'm sure others did not appreciate it. However, in principle he really had little choice. Wesley's aim was to present, from a large collection of works, the cream of what he felt important for the average Christian reader. I, too, have taken such an approach to these prayers for every day of the week. I've omitted passages in the interest of time for the one praying the prayers. We live in a hectic world, and at first glance, the original form of these prayers is quite overwhelming. My aim is to encourage you to learn a pattern of prayer, which, in turn, becomes your own. This aim, of course, would quickly fall by the wayside if one became over-whelmed by the quantity of material.

During the next 60 days, may God truly bless you as you begin opening His wonderful *Window of Grace.*

A Collection of Prayers

A Collection of Forms of Prayer
for Every Day in the Week
(First printed in 1733)

General questions which may be used every morning.

1) Did I think of God first and last?

2) Have I examined how I behaved since last night's retirement?

3) Am I resolved to do all the good I can this day and to be diligent in the business of my calling?

General questions to ask before beginning evening devotions.

1) With what degree of attention and enthusiasm did I use my morning prayers, public or private?

2) Have I done anything without a present, or at least a previous, perception of its direct or remote tendency to the glory of God?

3) Did I in the morning consider what particular virtue I was to exercise and what business I had to do in the day?

4) Have I been zealous to undertake and active in doing what good I could?

5) Have I interested myself any further in the affairs of others than charity required?

6) Have I, before I visited or was visited, considered how I might thereby give or receive improvement?

7) Have I mentioned any failing or fault of another when it was not necessary for the good of that person?

8) Have I unnecessarily grieved anyone by word or deed?

Sunday Morning Prayer

Behold the angels have gathered together in their choirs, and the saints are ready with their hymns. Behold the church prepares to worship Him and is now calling the community to come in and bring their praises.

I come now adoring my glorified Jesus.

The King of heaven Himself invites me and He graciously calls me up into His presence. You call me to put aside all the distractions of my daily life so I can think on You alone. To You I owe all the days of my life. I cheerfully enter into Your presence, the place You have chosen for me to dwell. I humbly bow before You as You meet me and hear my prayers.

Almighty God, Father of all mercies, I now present myself with all humility before You to offer my morning prayers of love and thanksgiving. Glory be to You, most adorable Father, Who, after finishing the work of creation, entered into a day of rest. Glory be to You, O holy Jesus, Who having through the Spirit offered Yourself a full, perfect and sufficient sacrifice for the sins of the whole world. You rose again the third day from the dead and had all power given to You both in heaven and on earth. Glory be to You, Holy Spirit, Who, proceeding from the Father and the Son, came down in tongues of fire on the apostles on the first day of the week, enabling them to preach the good news of salvation to a broken and dying world. Glory be to You, O holy and undivided Trinity, for working together in the great work of redemption, and restoring us once again to the glorious liberty of the sons of God. Glory be to You, Who, in compassion to human weakness, has appointed a day for the remembrance of the great benefits of following Jesus.

Dear Lord, I give You praise for the great privilege and happiness I have in knowing this day is set apart for the concerns of my soul. This is a day free from distractions, disengaged from the world. I have nothing but praise and love for You. May this day always be to me one set aside for rest and refreshment in You.

Dear Father, let your Holy Spirit, Who on the first day of the week descended in miraculous gifts on the apostles, descend on me, Your humble servant, that I may be always in the spirit on the Lord's day. Let His inspiration ... assist me in all the duties of this Your holy day. May my thoughts not wander from you, Lord; help me to seek You throughout the day. Let me join in the prayers and praises of Your church with heavenly affection. May I hear Your Word with earnest attention and a fixed resolution to obey it. And when I approach Your altar, pour into my heart humility, faith, hope, love. May I give this whole day to the ends for which it was set aside in works of necessity and mercy, in prayer, praise and meditation, and may "the words of my mouth, and the meditation of my heart, be always acceptable in Your sight."

I know that You have commanded me, and therefore it is my duty, to love You with all my heart and with all my strength. I know You are infinitely holy and overflowing in all perfection, and therefore it is my duty to love You.

I know You have created me, and that I have neither being nor blessing, except for what You give by Your goodness.

I know You are the end for which I was created, and that I can expect no happiness except happiness which comes from You.

I know that in love to me, being lost in sin, You did send

Your only Son, and that He, being the Lord of glory, humbled Himself to suffer death on a cross, so that He would be raised again in glory.

I know that You have provided me with all necessary helps for carrying me through this life to that eternal glory of heaven, and this out of the excess of Your pure mercy to me.

Upon these, and many other mercies and acts of your love, I now confess it is my duty to love You, my God, with all my heart. Give Your strength unto Your servant, that Your love may fill my heart and be the motive of all that I do. Dear Lord, let this rule my heart without a rival. Let love be the motive of all my thoughts, words and works. I love You with all my heart, and mind, and soul and strength.

Dear Lord, confirm Your past mercies to me, by enabling me, for what remains of my life, to be more faithful to You than I have been in the past. Let me not trust in words, or sighs, or tears, but may I trust in Your love. May I feel Your love in my heart, and then I will know what it is to love You with all my heart.

O merciful Father, whatever You do, do not deny me this love. Save me from the idolatry of loving the world or any of the things of the world. Let men never love any creature more than You. Take full possession of my heart. Being created by You, let me live for You. Being created by You, let me always act in a way bringing glory to You. Being saved by You, let me give back to You what is Yours, and let my spirit always be one with Yours.

Dear Father, may the prayers of Your church offered this day be graciously accepted. Clothe those in ministry leadership with righteousness this day. Bless those ministers who proclaim Your truth today. *(Name pastors, Sunday school teachers and others in ministry.)* Enable us of this nation, and especially those whom You have set over us in the church, to serve You in all holiness and to know the love of Christ which passes all understanding. Pour down Your blessing on our Christian educational system, so that it will always promote true religion and sound teaching. Show mercy, dear Lord, to my father and mother, my brothers and sisters, and to all my friends. *(Remember these people by name.)* Also, dear Lord, I pray for my relatives and my enemies. May You bless those I know. Let Your Fatherly hand be over them, and may Your Holy Spirit be with them. May they submit themselves entirely to Your will, and direct all their thoughts, words, and works to Your glory, so that they and those that are already dead in the Lord, may at length enjoy You in the glories of Your kingdom, through Jesus Christ our Lord, Who lives, and reigns with You and the Holy Spirit, one God, blessed forever.

Sunday Evening Prayer

Particular questions relative to the love of God.

1) Have I set apart some of this day to think upon His perfections and mercies?

2) Have I worked to make this day a day of heavenly rest set aside for God?

3) Have I employed those parts of it in works of necessity and mercy, which were not employed in prayer, reading and meditation?

All is unquiet until we come to You. When we enter into Your presence, we find peace. You are the victorious conqueror of sin and death. You are the refresher of our distressed spirits. Make us thirst and sigh after You, the living fountain of life-giving streams. May I focus all my attention on You, Lord, since nothing can satisfy my soul but You. Let my soul seek nothing but You.

Dear Father, I rejoice because I know I am in Your hand. Do with me what seems good in Your sight. Only let me love You with all my mind, soul and strength. I praise Your name for saving me and teaching me of Your ways in Your doctrine of truth and holiness. I praise Your name for Your gracious providence and guiding me by Your Spirit, for admitting me, with the rest of my Christian friends, to come before You during public worship. I thank You for so often feeding my soul and giving me a sense of assurance of Your forgiveness, which gives both strength and comfort. Strengthen my heart, I pray, in Your ways against all temptations and make me more than a conqueror in Your love.

Dear Father, deliver me from too intense an application to even necessary business. I know how this takes my thoughts from the one end of all my business, which is seeking You at all times. I know the narrowness of my heart, and that an eager attention to things around me leaves no room to think on the things of heaven. Teach me to go through all the events of my day seeing You in all things.

Deliver me, Father, from a wandering mind and from all lukewarmness. I know these deaden my love for You. Mercifully free my heart from them and give me a lively, zealous, active and cheerful spirit.

Deliver me, Father, from all idolatrous love of any creature. I know many have been lost by loving something other than You with all their heart. May I never open my heart to anything but out of love to You. Above all, deliver me from all idolatrous self-love. I know You made me, not to do my own will, but Yours.

Dear Lord, send Your Holy Spirit into the midst of the world and make us a holy people. Stir up the heart of our political leaders and those in ministry. Comfort those who are sick and hurting, and may their trial strengthen their faith in You. Be near *(name those who are sick and in need of prayer)*.

Change the hearts of my enemies, and give me the grace to

forgive them, even as You, for Christ's sake, forgave us.

Dear Lord, keep me safe this night, watching over me with Your eye of protection, and I will continually sing the praise of God the Father, God the Son, and God the Holy Spirit throughout all ages, world without end.

> "Our Father who art in heaven,
> Hallowed be thy name.
> Thy kingdom come.
> Thy will be done
> in earth as *it is* in heaven.
> Give us this day our daily bread.
> And forgive us our debts,
> as we forgive our debtors.
> And lead us not into temptation,
> but deliver us from evil:
> For thine is the kingdom, and the
> power and glory, fore ever.
> Amen" (Matthew 6:9-13, KJV).

Monday Morning Prayer

With reverence I appear before You, O Lord, and I humble myself in the presence of Your glory.

I come now adoring my God and Creator.

You made me and freely gave me all I see around. I give You praise for the glorious riches You give me each day. My body You framed from the dust of the earth, and gave me a soul after Your own likeness. A soul which all created nature cannot fill. You Yourself made me and for Your glorious kingdom, that I might dwell with You in perfect harmony, singing Your praises forever.

Dear Father, You are the giver of all good gifts, and I, Your servant, desire to praise Your name for all the expressions of Your love toward me. Blessed be Your love for giving Your Son to die for my sins, for the means of grace, and for the hope of glory. Blessed be Your love for all the temporal benefits You have poured out on me. For my health and strength, food and clothes, and all other necessities You have provided me throughout my life.

I also praise Your name, that even in my stubbornness, You still have patience with me and have watched over me through the night and given me yet another day to renew and perfect my faith and trust in You. Forgive me, Lord, of all my former sins, and make me every day more zealous and diligent to improve every opportunity of building up my soul in Your faith, love and obedience. Make Yourself always present in my mind, and let Your love fill and rule my soul in all those places, companies and tasks to which You call me this day. As I live in this world, may You help me not to set my heart upon it. Help me, Father, to always look to You with my undivided attention seeking the "prize of the high calling." This one thing let me do, let me press toward the prize so that I'll be ready to meet You one day.

Dear Lord, help me to show all those I encounter the same loving-kindness You show to all humankind. May I treat all my neighbors with that tender love which is due to Your servants and to Your children. You have required this mark of my love to You, and let no temptation expose me to ingratitude or make me forfeit Your loving-kindness which is better than life itself. Help me, Father, to assist all my fellow Christians with my prayers, where I cannot be with them in actual services. Make me zealous to embrace all occasions that may administer to their happiness by assisting the needy, protecting the oppressed, instructing the students, confirming the wavering, exhorting the good and reproving the wicked. Let me look upon the failings of my neighbor as if they were my own, that I may be grieved by them, that I may never reveal them, except when charity requires and then with tenderness and compassion.

Dear Lord, let Your love to me be the pattern of my love to the Father. You thought nothing too dear to part with to rescue me from eternal misery. Let me think nothing too dear to part with to set forward the everlasting good of my fellow Christians. They are members of Your body, therefore I cherish them.

Extend, I humbly ask, Your mercy to all humankind, and let them become faithful servants. Let all Christians live up to the holy religion they profess. Be favorable to Your people and continue to pour out Your grace upon the nation. Defend the church from schism, heresy and sacrilege. Protect our political leaders and all those in Christian ministry.

Preserve my parents, brothers and sisters, my friends and relations, and all humankind in their souls and bodies. *(Name family and friends.)* Forgive my enemies, and in Your due time make them kindly affected towards me. Have mercy on all who are sick. Give them patience under their sufferings and a happy issue out of all their pains. Grant that we, with those who are already dead in Your faith and fear, may together take part in a joyful resurrection through Him Who lives and reigns with You and the Holy Spirit, one God, world without end. Amen.

Monday Evening Prayer

Questions relating to the love of our neighbor.

1) Have I thought anything but my conscience too dear to part with, to please or serve my neighbor?

2) Have I rejoiced or grieved with him?

3) Have I received his infirmities with pity, not with anger?

4) Have I contradicted anyone, either where I had no good end in view, or where there was no probability of convincing?

5) Have I let him, whom I thought in the wrong, have the last word?

To know You, O Lord, is the highest learning, and to see Your face is the only happiness. I thankfully remember who You are. You are the great Beginning of our nature and the glorious End of all my actions. You are the overflowing Source from where I spring and the immense Ocean to which I tend. You are the free Giver of all I possess and the faithful Promiser of all I hope. You are the strong Sustainer of my life and the ready Deliverer from all my enemies. You are the merciful Forgiver of all my sins and the bounteous Rewarder of my obedience. You are the safe Conductor of my journey and the eternal Rest of my tired soul.

Most great and glorious Lord God, I humbly bow before Your throne of grace. Accept my imperfect repentance and send Your Spirit of adoption into my heart. I offer to You tonight my humblest thanks for watching over me this day. If I have escaped any sin, it is from the effect of Your restraining grace. If I have avoided any danger, it was Your hand that directed me. I give You all the praise and the glory You deserve tonight for keeping me safe this day.

Dear Father, fill my soul with so entire a love of You that I will love nothing but for Your sake. Give me grace to study Your knowledge daily that the more I know of You, the more I will love You. Create in me a zealous obedience to all Your commands, a cheerful patience under all Your chastisements, and a thankful resignation to all You send my way. Let it be the one business of my life to glorify You by every thought of my heart, by every word of my tongue, by every work of my hand, by professing Your truth, even to the death, if it should please You to call me to it now. In all that I do Lord, may it bring glory and honor to You.

Let Your unwearied and tender love to me make my love unwearied and tender to my neighbor. Make me peaceful and teachable, easy to forgive and glad to return good for evil.

Dear Lord, I pray tonight for protection over my father and mother, brothers and sisters, my friends and relatives and my enemies. Refresh me with such a comfortable rest that I will rise in the morning more fit for your service. Let me lie down with holy thoughts of You, and when I wake in the morning, let me be still present with You.

Show mercy to the whole world, Father, and let the gospel of Your Son run and be glorified throughout all the earth. Let Your Word be known among all people. Be merciful to the church and nation. May You give those in Christian ministry a discerning spirit that they may make proper choices as they seek Your face. *(Name pastors and other church leaders.)* Enable all who are ordained to any church office to diligently feed those people committed to them, instructing them in saving knowledge, guiding them by their examples, praying for and blessing those around them, exercising spiritual discipline in Your church and faithfully growing in You every day.

Send Your Spirit of healing to all those who are sick tonight. *(Name those who are sick.)* Lighten their burdens, Father, giving them a cheerful heart. I pray all of these things giving glory and honor to the Father, and to the Son, and to the Holy Spirit. Amen.

Tuesday Morning

From You, O Lord, I derive my being, and this morning I come adoring You, the God Who preserves me. You protect me from all my enemies and the dangers of the day. You send Your grace to relieve my weakness. I praise You for Your almighty power which sustains my life and Your mercy giving me space to repent.

O eternal and merciful Father, I give You humble thanks for all the blessings, spiritual and temporal, which in the riches of Your mercy, You have poured out on me. Lord, let me not live but to love You and to glorify Your name. Particularly, I give You thanks for protecting me from my birth to this point in my life and for bringing me safely to the beginning of this day. I ask that all my thoughts, words and works will give You glory. Heal, O Father of mercies, all my infirmities *(name your areas of sickness),* strengthen me against all my temptations and forgive me of all my sins. *(Name areas requiring forgiveness.)* Dear Lord, let my shortcomings not cry louder in Your ears than my prayers for mercy and forgiveness.

Dear Lord, I ask that You would give me the mind which is in You. May I learn from You how to be meek, lowly and humble. Pour into me the whole spirit of humility; fill me, and every part of my soul with it, making it the constant, ruling habit of my mind. Grant that I may think of myself as I ought to think, that I may know myself, even as I am known. May I exercise myself continually in this fashion. When I lie down and when I rise up, may I always remain humble in spirit.

Convince me that I have neither learned wisdom, nor have the knowledge of the holy. Give me a lively sense that I am nothing, that I have nothing, and that I can do nothing without You. Save me from either desiring or seeking the honor that comes from man. Convince me that the words of praise, "when smoother than oil," are then especially "very swords." Give me to dread them more than poison or sickness that kills. And when these cords of pride, these snares of death do overtake me, help me not to take any pleasure in them but enable me instantly to run to You, O Lord, seeking help, strength and forgiveness. Let all my bones cry out, "You are worthy to be praised, so shall I be safe from my enemies," when I give all the praise and the glory back to You.

Bless, O gracious Father, all the nations You have placed on the earth with a knowledge of You, the one and only true God. Bless the church and fill it with truth and grace. Where it is corrupt, purge it; where it is in error, correct it; where it is right, confirm it. Where it is divided, heal it. Let all those who serve You be refreshed. Let their prayers be as precious incense in Your sight, that their cries and tears for the city of their God may not be in vain.

Have mercy on this nation, and forgive the sins of this people. Inspire the leaders to seek Your face. Pour down Your blessings on our Christian schools. Comfort those who are sick, especially those suffering for Your sake. Bless my father and mother, my brothers and sisters, my friends and relatives and all that belong to this family. Forgive all who are my enemies, and so reconcile them to me and Yourself that we all, together with those that now sleep in You, may awake to life everlasting, through Your merits and prayers.

Dear Lord, I give You all the praise and glory which only You deserve this day. Amen.

Tuesday Evening

Questions related to humility.

1) Have I labored to conform all my thoughts, words and actions to these fundamental maxims: "I am nothing, I have nothing, I can do nothing without you Lord"?

2) Have I set apart some time this day to think on my shortcomings and sins?

3) Have I ascribed to myself any part of any good which God did by my hand?

4)   Have I said or done anything with a view to the praise of men?

5)   Have I desired the praise of men?

6)   Have I taken pleasure in it?

7)   Have I commended myself, or others, to their faces, except for God's sake, and then with fear and trembling?

8)   Have I despised anyone's advice?

9)   Have I, when I thought so, said, "I am in the wrong?"

10) Have I omitted justifying myself where the glory of God was not concerned? Have I submitted to be thought in the wrong?

Dear Lord, I desire to offer to You my evening sacrifice, the sacrifice of a contrite spirit. Have mercy upon me, O God, after Your great goodness and after the multitude of Your mercies do away with my offences. Let Your unspeakable mercy free me from the sins I have committed this day and deliver me from the punishment I deserve. *(Name areas of your life needing forgiveness.)* Save me Lord from every work of darkness and cleanse me from all that separates me from You so that I may come to You now with a pure heart and mind, following You, the only true God.

O Lamb of God, Who, both by example and action, instructed us to be meek and humble, give me grace throughout my whole life, in every thought, and word and work, to imitate Your meekness and humility. Rid my whole body of pride, grant me to feel that I am nothing, have nothing, and that I deserve nothing. Remind me that all my strength comes from only You. Grant, O Lord, that I may look for nothing, claim nothing, and that I may go through all the scenes of life not seeking my own glory, but looking wholly unto You, and acting wholly for You. Let me never speak any word that may tend to my own praise, unless the good of my neighbor requires it, and even then let me beware as I could heal another, but wound my own soul.

Let my ears and my heart never hear the praise that comes from men, and let me refuse to hear the voice of the charmer, even though he charms ever so sweetly. Give me a dread of applause, in whatever form it may come. I know that many stronger men have been slain by it, and that it leads only to destruction and death of the soul. Dear Lord, deliver my soul from this snare of hell, and help me not to spread it for the feet of others.

You are the Giver of every good and perfect gift. If at any time it pleases You to work by my hand, teach me to discern what is my own from what is another's and to give to You all the things that are Yours. All the good that is done on earth is done by You; let me always return to You the glory You deserve. Let me, as a pure crystal, transmit all the light You pour into me unto those around me. But may I never claim the light as my own, because it all comes from You.

Dear Lord, You were despised and rejected by men, and when I am slighted by my friends, disdained by my superiors, ridiculed by my equals, or treated poorly by my inferiors, let me cry out as others have in the past, "It is now that I begin to be a disciple of Christ!" (Ignatius). Then let me thankfully accept, and faithfully use, the happy occasion of improving in Your humble and lowly spirit. If for Your sake others use my name for evil, let me rejoice and be glad.

Help me, Lord, to remember You while I sleep and to think on You when I awaken. You have protected me from all the dangers of this day, and You have been my support throughout my life up until now. Under the shadow of Your wings let me now pass this night in comfort and peace.

Dear Lord and Preserver of all humankind, have mercy on all the nations. Purge the church from all heresy, schism and superstition. Bless those in office over us both politically and spiritually. Pour on our whole church, especially the clergy, your continual blessing.

Bless all my relatives, especially my father and mother, my brothers and sisters, and all my friends. *(Name them.)* Turn the hearts of my enemies *(name them),* forgive them and me all our sins, and grant that we, and all the members of Your holy church, may find mercy through the mediation and satisfaction of Your blessed Son, Jesus Christ, to Whom, with You and the Holy Spirit, the Comforter, be all honor, praise and thanksgiving, forever and ever. Amen.

Wednesday Morning

You are my great and sovereign Lord, the absolute King in heaven and earth. You see at once all that takes place in this world. I humbly come before You, Lord, adoring You this morning. You appoint every creature to a fit office, and You guide all our motions in perfect order. You will continue doing this as You bring about Your design to finish the world in all its beauty. You govern with infinite wisdom and all for the good of those who love You. Your counsels and wisdom are deep and beyond our reach, but all Your ways are just and merciful. I praise You, Father, because You govern Your enemies with a rod of iron and punish their disobedience with justice. But Your servants, You treat as privileged children, and You provide for their eternity a rich inheritance.

Dear Lord, Who lives in the light which no man can approach, in whose presence there is no night, I, your humble servant, whom You preserved through the night, I give You praise and adoration today. I humbly pray that this and all the days of my life may be fully given to You and Your service. Send Your Holy Spirit, I pray, to be the guide of all my ways and the sanctifier of my soul and body. Save, defend and build me up in Your love. Give to me, I pray, the light of Your presence, peace from heaven and the salvation of my soul in the day of the Lord Jesus.

You, Who are the way, the truth and the life, have said that no man can follow You unless he renounces himself. I know You have not burdened me with anything I cannot handle this day which You deem necessary for my growth in You. Dear Lord, I know how You emptied Yourself of Your eternal glory and took upon Yourself the form of a servant among humankind. You, Who made all humankind to serve and please You, did not please Yourself, but became the servant of all. You, O Lord of all heaven and earth, turned the other cheek while being whipped and allowed Yourself to be nailed on a cross so that all might find life in You. My Lord and my God, may I never presume to be above You, my Master. May it be the one desire of my heart to be as my Master, to do not my own will, but the will of the Father Who sent me.

Dear Lord, give me the grace to walk after Your pattern and in Your steps. Give me the grace to "take up my cross daily" as I faithfully follow You and give me the grace to do the things that are pleasing in Your sight. You, who did not please Yourself, let some portion of Your Spirit fall on me that I may "deny myself and follow You." Strengthen my soul that I may be temperate in all things. May I never seek only my own pleasure; may I actually seek to only please You. Save me, Lord, from indulging either in earthly desires of the eye or the pride of life. Set a watch over my senses and appetites, my passions and understanding, that I may deny everything that brings glory to me. May I always seek to glorify Your name. Help me, Father, to live a holy life in this unholy world, living in the world, but not being of it.

Hear also my prayers for all humankind and guide their feet into the way of peace. I pray for the church; may it live by Your Spirit and reign in Your glory. Give to the church leaders and those in ministry Your wisdom and peace so that they may save both themselves and those they minister to.

Preserve, O great King of heaven and earth, our Christian political leaders. Give them the wisdom they require to faithfully serve You in the offices they represent. To all Your people give your heavenly grace, that they may faithfully serve You all the days of their lives. Bless the Christian schools with unity and holiness. May those who have fallen away from You remember that they are a "chosen people, a royal priesthood, a holy nation, called to be a holy people," and may You, Dear Lord, call them out of their darkness back into your light. I give to You once again this morning my father and mother, my brothers and sisters, as well as my friends and my relatives. (Name them.) Lord, You know best all their needs and wants, may You bless them accordingly.

Dear Father, let these my prayers find access to Your throne of grace, through the Son of Your love, Jesus Christ the Righteous One, to whom with You, in the unity of the Spirit, be all love and obedience now and forever. Amen.

Wednesday Evening

Questions related to humility.

1) Have I done anything merely because it was pleasing?
2) Have I looked for excuses to avoid self-denial? In particular ...
3) Have I submitted my will to the will of everyone that opposed it, except where the glory of God was concerned?

Dear Lord of heaven and earth, I humbly come before You confessing my shortcomings and sins. I confess that I have sinned against You by thought, word and deed, particularly this day. (Think about the *day, ask forgiveness in areas of need.)* I praise You, Father, because You are not only Judge, but You're also my Savior. Deliver me from the power of sin and temptation; preserve me and save me, I pray.

You, whose mercy is without measure, whose goodness is unspeakable, forgive me this day. May Your Spirit wash over me, making me clean and right before God. Help me to humbly walk with You in holiness. My Lord and my God, I know that unless I am planted together with You in Your likeness, I cannot be saved. Strengthen me so that by denying myself and taking up my cross daily, I may crucify the old self in me and live only for You. Give me grace to always look to You for guidance, denying all worldly desires and passions. Let me be dead to sin so that I might be holy through and through. Let me be dead to my will and alive only to Yours. I am not my own. You have bought me with the price of Your own blood. You died for all so that all may live. Make me a new creation in Your image. May Your Holy Spirit enable me to say with the Apostle Paul, "I am crucified with Christ. I no longer live, but He lives within me."

O Great Shepherd of souls, bring home to Your sheep pen all who've strayed away. Preserve Your church from all heresy and schism, and from all that persecutes or opposes the truth. Give to those in Christian ministry wisdom and holiness and the powerful aid of Your Holy Spirit. Advance the just and give them the grace to do Your will in the world and eternal glory in the world to come.

Dear Lord, bless our Christian schools that they may devote all their studies to Your glory. Have mercy on all who are sick, remember the poor and needy, the widow and the fatherless, the friendless and the oppressed. Heal the sick; give them a special touch of Your healing hand.

I praise You for Your continual preservation of me, and for Your fatherly protection over me throughout this day. For all the comforts that surround me this day, I give You praise. Accept these my prayers, O merciful Father, and may You keep watch over me through the night as I now prepare for rest. Amen.

Thursday Morning

O Eternal God, my Sovereign Lord, I acknowledge that all I am and all I have comes only from You. Give me such a sense of Your infinite goodness this day that I may give back to You all possible love and obedience.

I humbly and heartily thank You for all the favors You have given me. For creating me after Your own image, for Your daily preserving me by Your providence, for saving me from death, by the very death of Your Son, Jesus Christ, and for the assistance of Your Holy Spirit. I praise You for causing me to be born in a Christian country, for blessing me with a means of salvation, and with religious parents and friends. I also thank You for all your earthly blessings and for bringing me safely through another night. I praise You and thank You for my health, strength, food, clothes and all the other comforts of living. May I always remember to praise Your name for all You do for me.

Dear Father of mercies, may You always look toward me with compassion. I humbly ask Your forgiveness for all my sins. I come now to do Your will, and by Your assistance I will live a life pleasing to You. Help me, Lord, to always seek to obey You while praying, "Father, not my will, but Your will be done." You, O Lord, are above all, through all and in all. In You I live and have my being. May my will be entirely and continually derived from Yours, just as my continuous happiness and joy come only from You.

I humbly ask You this morning to teach me to adore all

Your ways, even though I cannot comprehend them. Teach me to be glad that You are King and to give You thanks for all things that come my way. For that which is about to come my way, may You give me the grace to do in all things that which pleases You, and then, with an absolute submission to Your wisdom, may I leave the issues in Your hand.

Dear Lord, I give You my body, my soul, my being, my fame, my friends, my liberty and my life! Use me and all that is in me as You see best. I am not mine, but Yours. Claim me as Your right, keep me as Your charge, love me as Your child. Fight for me when I am assaulted, heal me when I am wounded, and revive me when I am destroyed.

Help me with Your grace, that whatever I may do or suffer this day, that it will all be done to Your glory. Keep me in love to You and all humankind. Direct my footsteps this day and help me to always remain in touch with You.

Extend Your grace to all humankind. May many see Your love and come to accept Your truth this day. Be gracious to the church, and help those in ministry to always preserve the doctrine and discipline You have delivered. Grant that all Your servants may bring You glory and honor this day. Bless all the Christian schools and let them not neglect their task of teaching. Be merciful to all who are in distress or that struggle with pain or poverty. Be a guide to all those who travel today. Give a strong and quiet spirit to those who are condemned to death and liberty to the prisoners.

Give spiritual strength and comfort to all who need it and salvation to those who understand. Give to all that are in error the light of your truth. Bring all sinners to repentance *(name those who need to accept Christ)* and unite us all to one another by mutual love, and to Yourself in constant holiness, that we, together with all those who are gone before us in Your faith and fear may find merciful acceptance in the last day through the merits of Your blessed Son, to whom with You and the Holy Spirit be all glory and honor. Amen.

Thursday Evening

Questions relating to resignation and meekness.

1) Have I endeavored to will what God wills, and that only?

2) Have I received everything that has come to me this day without my choice with thanks?

3) Have I (after doing what He requires of me to do concerning them) left all future things absolutely to God's disposal? That is, have I left all my concerns and burdens in His hands?

4) Have I resumed my claim to my body, soul, friends, fame or fortune, which I have made over to God, or taken my gift back, when God accepted any of them at my hands?

5) Have I endeavored to be cheerful, mild and courteous in whatever I said or did?

6) Have I said anything with a stern look, accent or gesture? Particularly with regard to Christianity?

Who will give me this happy favor that I may find God alone? That I may find Him in the silence of preparing for a night's rest, where the noise of this world cannot interrupt us. I wish to unfold before Him my wants and ask for His counsel. What shall I do, gracious Lord, to be happy with You? I seek Your wise counsel and advice. Let every word sink deep into my soul. May I hunger and thirst only after You. May my whole soul seek You alone, since You alone are all I need.

My Lord and my God, You see my heart, and my desires

are not hidden from You. I am encouraged by my happy experience of Your goodness, and I now present myself before You. I am ashamed when I think of how long I lived a stranger to You. But I now praise Your name, because You invited me to return to Your side. I know I am nothing and can do nothing by myself. O my God, my Savior, my Sanctifier, turn not away Your face from a poor soul like mine who seeks You. Lord hear me, help me and show mercy to me for Jesus Christ's sake.

To You, O God, Father, Son and the Holy Spirit, my Creator, Redeemer and Sanctifier, I give up myself entirely. May I no longer serve myself, but serve You all the days of my life. I give You my understanding. May it be my only care to know You, Your perfections, Your works and Your will. Let all other things fall away so that I may totally give myself to You.

I give You my will. May I have no will except Your own. May I will Your glory in all things and may I sing with the Psalmist, "Who have I in heaven but You, and there is no one else on earth that I desire more than You." May I find happiness in doing Your will at all times. Whatever threatens me, may I say, "It is the Lord, let Him do what seems good to Him." And whatever comes my way, let me always give thanks, since it is Your will concerning me.

I give You my affections. May You be my one true love, my fear, my joy, and may nothing have any share of them. What You love, may I also love. What You hate, may I also hate. I give to You my body. May I glorify You with it and preserve it holy, fit for You and Your service. May I neither indulge it, nor use too much rigor towards it. May I always keep it healthy, vigorous and active, and fit to do Your will in all manner of service which You call me for. I give You all my worldly goods. May I prize them and use them only for You. May I faithfully restore to You, in the poor, all You have entrusted to me.

I give You credit for my reputation. May I never value it but only in respect of You. May I never endeavor to maintain it, but as it may do You service and advance Your honor in the world. I give You myself and my all. Let me look upon myself as to be nothing and to have nothing outside of You.

Dear Lord, whenever I am tempted to break my solemn promise with You, when I am pressed to conform to the world and to the company and customs that surround me, may my answer be, "I am not my own. I am not for myself, nor for the world but for my God." I will give to God the things which are God's.

Have mercy, dear Lord, on all humankind. Bless the church, heal its breaches and establish it in truth and peace. Preserve and defend all those in Christian ministry and bless them with sound doctrine and purity of life. Bless the Christian schools with learning and holiness that they may graduate a constant supply of people fit and able to do your service.

Shower down Your graces on all my relations, on all my friends and on all that belong to this family. Comfort and relieve those that labor under any affliction of body or mind. Visit them, O gracious Lord, in all their distresses. Those that love or do good to me, reward them greatly. (Name those who help you.) Those that hate me (name those who hate you), convert and forgive, and grant us all, together with Your whole church, an entrance into your kingdom through Jesus Christ, to whom with You, and the Holy Spirit, three Persons, and one God, I give all majesty, praise and thanksgiving. Amen.

Friday Morning

I come before You this morning, Father, with adoration and praise for Your redeeming grace. When I had sold myself to sin and had become a slave to Satan, You sent Your Son, Jesus Christ, from heaven, Who paid a high price to buy my freedom. The price was no less than His own blood, which He shed freely on the cross to rescue me from eternal death. I now give this day to His precious memory, thanking Him for all He did for me. Help me, Father, to set aside all distractions so my prayers might mount more swiftly to heaven.

Almighty and everlasting God, I praise You from my heart that Your goodness preserved me and protected me throughout this past night. I pray that Your protection will stay close throughout this day. I humbly ask You to watch over me with Your eyes of mercy. Direct my soul and body according to the rule of Your will, and fill my heart with Your Holy Spirit, so that I might pass through this day, and all the rest of my days to Your glory.

O Savior of the world, God of Gods, Light of light, You are the brightness of Your Father's glory, the express image of His person. You have destroyed the power of the devil and overcome death, and You now sit at the right hand of the Father. May You be my light and my peace. Destroy the power of the devil in me and make me a new creature. You, Who cast out seven spirits from Mary Magdalene, cast out of my heart all evil desires. You, Who raised Lazarus from the dead, raise me from the death of sin. You, Who cleansed the lepers, healed the sick and gave sight to the blind, heal the diseases of my soul. Open my eyes and fix them only on the prize of my high calling and cleanse my heart from every desire except that of advancing Your glory.

Dear Lord, You were unknown and despised while walking on this earth. Have mercy on me, Lord, and let me not be ashamed to follow You. Dear Jesus, You were hated and persecuted while on this earth. Have mercy on me and let me not be ashamed to come after You. Dear Lord, You were betrayed and sold by one of Your own disciples. Have mercy on me and make me content to be as my Master. Dear Jesus, You were ridiculed, accused and wrongfully sentenced to death on a cross. Have mercy on me and teach me to endure the ridicule I suffer for living my life for You. Dear Jesus, You did nothing to seek Your own glory; You lived bringing glory to the Father in heaven. Have mercy on me and let me not seek my own glory. Dear Jesus, You were insulted, mocked and spit upon. Have mercy on me and let me run with patience the race set before me.

Dear Jesus, You were dragged to a pillar, beaten and bathed in Your blood. Have mercy on me and let me not grow faint in the fiery trials of life. Dear Jesus, You were crowned with thorns and hailed as king in a joking manner. You were burdened with my sins and the sins of the people. You hung on a cross, bowing Your head and giving up Your very spirit for me. Have mercy and conform my whole soul to your holy, humble and suffering Spirit. Dear Lord, for the love of me, You went through many sufferings and humiliations. May I be wholly emptied of myself so I might rejoice and take up my cross daily while following You. Enable me to endure the pain and despise the shame, and, if it be Your will, to resist even by the shedding of my own blood.

Holy, holy, holy, Lord God Almighty, I humbly acknowledge that I am altogether unworthy to pray for myself. But since You have commanded me to make prayers and intercession for all humankind, in obedience to Your command, and confidence of Your unlimited goodness, I commend to Your mercy the wants and needs of all humankind. Lord, may it be Your good pleasure to restore to the church peace and purity. May You show mercy to the sinful nations and give us grace at length to break off our sins by asking for Your forgiveness. Defend the church from all the assaults of schism and heresy and bless all those in Christian ministry and leadership.

Dear Father, may it be Your good pleasure to give Your grace to our Christian schools. Bless those whom I have wronged (*name people you've offended in any way*). Forgive those who have wronged me (*name people who've hurt you in any way*). Dear Lord, give health and patience to all that are sick (*name those sick and in hospital*).

Protect and bless my parents. May they sense Your presence throughout this day. Let them remember how short their time is and be careful to improve every moment of it. Dear Lord, You have kept them from their youth up until now; now that they are gray-headed, may Your protection continue with them. Perfect them in every good word and work and be their guide until death. Bless my brothers and sisters, whom You have graciously taught the gospel of Jesus Christ. Give them further degrees of illumination so they might serve You with a perfect heart and a willing mind. Bless my friends and all who have commended themselves to my prayers. (*Name those who are praying for you.*) Dear Lord, You know all our conditions, desires and wants. Bless us as You see fit.

Dear Father, I pray that You will hear my prayers and, for the sake of Your Son Jesus, bring me, with all those who have pleased You from the beginning of the world, into the glories of Your Son's kingdom, to whom, along with You and the Holy Spirit, receive my continual praise, now and forever. Amen.

Friday Evening

See questions before prayers for Wednesday evening.

Dear Lord, I come before You this night putting aside all the thoughts of the day. Help me now to examine this day, discovering if I've given You the glory, honor and praise.

O holy, blessed and glorious Trinity, Whom in three Persons I adore as one God, have mercy on me. Dear Lord, remember how short my time is and deliver not my soul into the power of hell. Let me live in Your sight. Let me live, dear Lord, and my soul shall praise You. Forgive me when I have been disobedient, and regard me as I am distressed, crying out to You for help. Consider me as Your created being and forgive me of all my sins. Dear Lord, how easy it is for You to forgive! For it is Your very nature. How proper it is for You to save! For it is Your very name. How suitable it is for You to come into the world! For it is Your business. Dear Father, have mercy on me.

I ask not of You the things of this world. All I ask this evening is that You would say to me, "Be of good cheer. Your sins are forgiven." Help me, dear Lord, never to sin against You again. Save me and receive me as a sheep that has gone astray. I now humbly return to the great Shepherd and Bishop of my soul.

Father, accept my imperfect repentance and forgive my wickedness. Purify my uncleanness, strengthen my weaknesses, fix my unstableness and let Your good Spirit watch over me now and forever. May Your love always rule in my heart, and may I in turn show this love to others around me.

Give Your grace, dear Lord, to all the world and let all who are saved by Your blood acknowledge You to be the Lord of all. Let all Christians keep themselves clean from the world. Let those in Christian ministry be exemplary in their lives and discreet and diligent in their work. Be a help to all who are sick and help them to trust in You. Raise up friends for the widows and fatherless, the friendless and oppressed. Give patience to all that are sick, comfort to all troubled in consciences, strength to all that are tempted. Be gracious to my relatives *(name them)*. Bless all who are endeared to me by their kindness, to all who remember me in their prayers, or desire to be remembered in mine. *(Name people who come to mind at this point.)* Sanctify, dear Lord, the friendship You have given me with my Christian colleagues. Let our prayers be heard for each other, while our hearts are united in love. Strengthen our hearts against all sin and temptations, enabling us to serve You faithfully.

Dear Father, by Your infinite mercies, keep us safe through this night and all the days of our lives, and bring us, with those who are already dead in You, to rejoice together before You, through the merits of our Lord Jesus Christ, to Whom, with You and the Holy Spirit, the King of kings, and the Lord of lords, be honor and power forever and ever. Amen.

Saturday Morning

I come singing praises and adoration to my victorious Redeemer! I give praise to the Prince of peace, to the Prince of my salvation and to the Lord of lords. You triumphed over death in your own body, and that in turn enables me to conquer it in mine; impart to me Your heavenly skill, giving me courage with infinite rewards. Let me live and die in Your blessed obedience, and may no temptation separate me from You, so that one day I might receive the crown of peace.

Dear Father, You are the Creator and Sovereign Lord of heaven and earth. You are the Father of angels and men; You are the Giver of life, and Protector of all Your creation. Mercifully accept this my morning sacrifice of praise and thanksgiving, which I now offer to You with all humility.

Everything You created sings out to You. The sun rejoices to run its course setting forth Your praise. The moon and the stars manifest Your glory even in the midst of a silent night. The earth breathes each day of Your beauty and presence. The floods clap their hands, and the hills are joyful together before You. You made light for our comfort and darkness so all living creatures might find rest. Pour Your grace into my heart this day, I pray, so I might magnify Your great and glorious name. You made me and sent me into the world to do Your work. Assist me to fulfill the end of my creation, and to show all those around me Your praise and love.

Protect me, Father, from those temptations which continually come after me and offend You. Guide me by Your Holy Spirit in all the places You will lead me today, and may my mind always be on You. Let me always walk in Your sight neither cold nor lukewarm. May I serve You with all my heart. Keep me safe throughout the day so I may diligently perform Your will wherever You lead.

Dear Lord, hear also my prayers for all humankind. Guide their feet into the way of peace. Reform the corruptions of Your church, heal divisions and restore her to holiness. Give to those in Christian ministry and leadership grace, as good shepherds, to feed the flocks committed to their charge.

I ask that You will be gracious to my father and mother, my brothers and sisters, and all my friends and relatives. Give them the share of blessings of this life that are good for them.

O gracious Comforter, be near those who are sick and in need of a special touch this day. Give to my enemies grace and forgiveness and help me to always show them Your love. Remove the cloud from their eyes and the stones from their hearts, that they may know and feel what it is to love their neighbors as themselves. Help me to love all my enemies and bless them that do me harm. Help me to do good to them that hate me, and to pray for those who despitefully use me and persecute me.

Dear Lord, lead, guide and direct me through this day, always seeking to bring glory, honor and praise to Your name, now and forever. Amen.

Saturday Evening

Questions relating to thankfulness.

1) Have I set aside some time for thanking God for the blessings of the past week?

2) Have I, in order to be more aware of them, taken time to seriously consider all that has happened to me and given praise to God for all that has happened this week?

O most great and glorious God, I come before You with thanksgiving and praise for my creation, protection through this day, and all the other blessings which, in the riches of Your mercy, You have from time to time poured out on me. You, Lord, in the beginning laid the foundation of the earth, and the heavens are the works of Your hand. You created the sun and the moon, the day and the night. You formed humankind from the dust of the ground, and breathed into him the breath of life. In Your own image You made him capable of knowing and loving You eternally. In the beginning, his nature was perfect; Your will was his law. Even after leaving the garden, You have not totally withdrawn Your mercy from him. In every succeeding generation, You have saved, assisted and protected Your creation. You have instructed us by Your laws and enlightened us by Your commandments. You have saved us by the blood of Your Son, and sanctified us by the grace of Your Holy Spirit. For these and all Your other mercies, how can I ever sufficiently love You, or worthily magnify Your great and glorious name? All the powers of my soul are too few to conceive the thanks that are due to You.

But You have declared it Your will to accept my praise and thanksgiving this hour. I will therefore always praise Your name, and I will forever adore Your power and thank You for Your goodness. I will sing of Your righteousness and tell of Your salvation all the days of my life. I will give thanks to You for ever and ever. I will praise my God all the days of my life. While I am on this earth, I will praise You as I can, the King of heaven. Even though I am a feeble and mortal creature, I will join my song with those that excel in strength, with the immortal choirs of angels singing Your praises all the day long.

Holy, holy, holy, is the Lord God of hosts! Heaven and earth are full of His glory! Glory be to You, O Lord most high. Amen. Hallelujah.

Accept, O merciful Father, my most humble thanks for Your protection this day. Dear Lord, continue Your loving-kindness toward me and take me into Your protection this night. Let Your holy angels watch over me to defend me from the attempts of evil men and evil spirits. Let me rest in peace and not sleep in sin. Grant that I might rise in the morning more fit and ready for Your service.

Dear Lord, Your kingdom rules over all. May it also rule in the hearts of all humankind. Reform the corruptions and heal the wounds in Your church. May You establish Your church in truth and peace. Be gracious to those in Christian ministry. Forgive the sins of this nation and turn our hearts to You and You alone. Bless our political leaders, and may they know You are in control.

Be gracious, Lord, to all who are near and dear to me. You know their names and are aware of their wants. Of Your goodness, be pleased to give to them their necessities. Forgive my enemies and give them repentance and charity and give me grace to overcome evil with good. Have compassion on all who are distressed in mind, body or spirit and give them steady patience and timely deliverance.

Now to God the Father, Who first loved us, and made us acceptable in His sight, to God the Son, Who loved us, and robed us in His righteousness by the shedding of His own blood, and to God the Holy Spirit, Who fills our hearts with the love of God, keep me safe this night. I give You praise and glory, now and forever, Amen.

Suggestions for Further Reading

This, of course, is not an attempt to give a complete list of resources in the area of John Wesley and prayer. However, this list does represent some books I've found helpful through the years.

A Collection of Forms of Prayers for Every Day of the Week, John Wesley, United Methodist Publishing House, 1992, 83 pages.

A Serious Call to a Devout and Holy Life, William Law, London: Dent, 1906, 355 pages.

Complete Works of E.M. Bounds on Prayer, E.M. Bounds, Baker Books, 1990, 576 pages.

Daily Wesley, Donald E. Demaray, Bristol House, 1993, 448 pages.

Devotional Life in the Wesleyan Tradition, Steve Harper, Upper Room, 1983, 80 pages.

Imitation of Christ, Thomas á Kempis, Catholic Book Publishing Co., 1941, 432 pages.

Meaning of Prayer, Harry Emerson Fosdick, Association Press, 1949, 188 pages.

Wesley's Works, John Wesley, Baker Book House, 1978, 14-volume set.

Prayer Books

A Diary of Private Prayer, John Baillie, Charles Scribner's Sons, 1949, 135 pages.

Book of Common Prayer, Seabury Press, 1979, 1001 pages.

Minister's Prayer Book, John W. Doberstein, Fortress Press, 1986, 490 pages.

Prayers for Every Occasion, Don Sanford, Zondervan, 1957, 121 pages.

Prayers That Avail Much, Volumes 1 and 2, Word Ministries, Inc, Harrison House, 1989, 139 pages.

Resources Out of Print, But Available in Archives

Christian Library, John Wesley, England: Felix Farley, 1749, 50-volume set.

Devotions and Prayers of John Wesley, Donald E. Demaray, Baker Book House, 1957, 109 pages.

Journals and Letters of Francis Asbury, Francis Asbury, Epworth Press, 1958, 3-volume set.